Strategic Project Portfolio Management

Strategic Project Portfolio Management

Enabling a Productive Organization

Simon Moore

WILEY

John Wiley & Sons, Inc.

Published by John Wiley & Sons, Inc., Hoboken, New Jersey.
Published simultaneously in Canada.

For general information on our other products and services, or technical support, please contact our Customer Care Department within the United States at 800-762-2974, outside the United States at 317-572-3993 or fax 317-572-4002.

Wiley also publishes its books in a variety of electronic formats. Some content that appears in print may not be available in electronic books.

For more information about Wiley products, visit our Web site at http://www.wiley.com.

Library of Congress Cataloging-in-Publication Data:

Moore, Simon, 1978–
Strategic project portfolio management : enabling a productive organization / Simon Moore.
    p.   cm. – (Microsoft executive leadership series ; 16)
Includes index.
Summary: "Lead change through strategic alignment of project and process performance Practical and filled with expert advice, Strategic Project Portfolio Management: Enabling a Productive Organization presents a clear framework for your organization to complete impactful strategic projects. Providing executive-level guidance to build a powerful and efficient process from initial adoption to portfolio alignment, this essential resource contains case studies from small to global multinational organizations, arming you with the insights to ensure your strategic projects are given the resources they need to deliver business impact. This important guide Shows executives how to align their projects and processes with their business strategy for compelling competitive advantage Provides cases from best in class organizations, showing how they were able to achieve results by using processes outlined in the book Reveals how technology is the key to developing new collaborative platforms and innovative work management environments that have not been possible until now Defines a framework for assessing project portfolio management competence within your organization and driving momentum for compelling improvements Explores how to go beyond project portfolio management to a holistic work management system Strategic Project Portfolio Management: Enabling a Productive Organization offers the practical recommendations, guidance, and real world insights you need to immediately begin driving better project management strategy"—
Provided by publisher.
ISBN 978-0-470-48195-0
1. Portfolio management.   2. Strategic planning.   I. Title.
HG4529.5.M66   2010
658.4′012–dc22   2009025056

10   9   8   7   6   5   4   3   2   1

Contents

Microsoft Executive Leadership Series: Series Foreword

Today's world requires lifelong learning. The Microsoft Executive Leadership Series provides leaders with access to new ideas and perspectives, intended to inspire and to challenge—ideas that will help keep thoughts fresh and minds nimble. These ideas range from effective strategy to deploying an agile infrastructure. Information technology increasingly drives the evolution of business models, social norms, market expansion, even the very shape and nature of our institutions. Organizations that succeed in the future will differentiate themselves effectively on how well they use technology to navigate change, respond to challenges, and leverage new opportunities.

I talk nearly every day to executives and policy makers grappling with issues like globalization, workforce evolution, and the impact of technology on people and processes. The idea for this series came from those conversations—we see the series as a way to distill what we've learned as a company into actionable intelligence. The authors bring independent perspectives, expertise, and experience. We hope their insights will spark dialogues within organizations, among managers, and with policy makers about the critical relationship between people and technology in the workplace of tomorrow.

I hope you enjoy this title in the Microsoft Executive Leadership Series and find it useful as you plan for the expected and unexpected developments ahead. It's our privilege and our commitment to be part of that conversation.

DANIEL W. RASMUS
General Editor, Microsoft Executive Leadership Series

THE REASON FOR THIS BOOK

This book exists to fill a gap in the current literature on project and portfolio management (PPM). Much has been written around theory of PPM, and there are a number of more technical books on the nuts and bolts of PPM technology. This book ties the theory and technology together, primarily for an executive audience, with the goal of enabling a productive organization. Executives don't need to understand all the granular detail of the technology, but there is a need to understand the latest thinking in PPM and how far both the discipline and the technology has moved beyond the simple Gantt chart. This book looks at the latest developments in a dynamic field that is critical to organizational success.

The book also takes a real-world look at the challenges of PPM, using case studies throughout the chapters, and examines not just how PPM should be done, but maps out ways to get there using a measured and pragmatic approach.

How the Book Is Organized

The first four chapters highlight the benefits of project portfolio management. The first two chapters focus primarily on the high-level strategic perspective in terms of creation of business goals and alignment of projects to them. Chapters three and Four emphasis benefits from disciplined planning and cost focus.

Chapters five, six, and seven together serve as a guide for best practice implementation.

Chapters eight, nine, and ten expand on the prior chapters to explore the need for effective communications structures, people-centric processes, together with appropriate use of workflow, and process overall.

Chapter eleven takes a more theoretical look at project management, surveying the key perspectives.

Chapter twelve looks at future trends across project and portfolio management, combining a business and technology perspective.

Case studies and call-outs on topics of interest are positioned in the appropriate chapters.

THE VALUE TO THE READER

The Executive

Executives in relatively large organizations are the primary audience for this book. They will quickly be brought up to speed on the latest thinking and benefits on project and portfolio management, from strategic goal setting and alignment to the latest thinking on postmortem processes. The book shares insights from multiple disciplines, including psychology, to explore the most effective way to think about a project portfolio in an organization. They will understand how technology can be used to support these efforts and magnify the benefits of a well-functioning organization.

Case studies provide examples from different industries and geographies to highlight the real-world implementation and best practices around the concepts discussed.

Key questions at the end of each chapter provide a mechanism for the executive to tie the content in the chapter back to their organization, and references are provided for some of the more technical concepts discussed.

The IT Professional

The IT Professional will learn more about the business context of project portfolio technology and best practices for successful implementation from the numerous case studies. The range of the case studies provides a way of thinking about how systems can be refined and tailored to the needs of different groups and teams.

The final chapter discusses future changes in the project portfolio management discipline, while the later chapters examine the link between project portfolio management and other systems and tools.

The Project or Portfolio Manager

The book offers insight into the broader strategic context of project and portfolio management and ways to grow support and enthusiasm for both the process and technology within the organization. Case studies enable learning from other organizations, and the book contains a number of tips and tricks that the project or portfolio manager will find useful in their day-to-day role to align their work with the key goals of the business they support.

Acknowledgments

This book is dedicated to Jamie Morris for her tremendous support during my writing of this book. I started on this book before we were engaged, and by the time it goes to print, we should be married.

Many thanks to Henry Moore, who provided all the illustrations. Thanks especially to Joy Moore, Richard Moore, and Charles Moore for all their support.

Thanks to Julian Tydeman for writing Chapter 11.

Thanks, particularly, to those who spent time reviewing the manuscript, making numerous valuable suggestions: Lori Birtley, Magnus Holmlid, Rudi van den Berg, Denis Gaynor, Craig Kilford, James Butler, and the ever-resourceful Marc Gawley.

Thanks to everyone else who helped make this book possible through their enthusiasm, perspectives, and support: Tim Burgard, Stacey Rivera, Jan Shanahan, Sam Hickman, Juliana Aldous, Tom Tenazawa, Kris Tibbetts, Sam Guckenheimer, Hilary Long, Tad Haas, Christoph Fiessinger, Scott Gordon, Lisa Snyder, Rex Foxford, Jamie Eddis, Jill Campbell, Will Holmes, Anna Hatt, Gary Cooper, Sandeep Mangla, Lloyd Stanley, Richard Toledo, Geoff Russell, Doug McCutcheon, Stuart Brown, Peter Grady, Pontus Pettersson, Doug Slater, Brian Nowak, Seth Patton, Ludovic Haduc, Keshav Puttaswamy, Alice Wignall, James Hatt, Anthonie Wain, Oliver Mears, Hirotake Abe, Tatsuro Sako, Stuart Brown, Ben Chamberlain, and James Brooks.

Introduction

Organizations that outperform do so because of a combination of strong execution and great strategy. Lack of either results in failure. Effective portfolio management helps achieve outperformance, making your strategy real through organizational change. Significant advances in technology have made portfolio management an area where technology can enable a truly productive organization.

Project management is a challenging discipline, but relatively well understood. Realizing the full benefits of portfolio management is harder, partly because the technology has evolved in recent years so the opportunities for advancing portfolio management are not well understood, but also because implementing a portfolio management process can become complex. To minimize this complexity, it is necessary to approach portfolio management in a well-phased, results-oriented, and inclusive manner.

Portfolio management software is part of a larger business process, as is most enterprise software, and to be broadly successful, portfolio management must reflect that broader process. No one expects software alone to create organizational change, but the challenge of introducing portfolio management within an organization is often underestimated and oversimplified. Knowing where technology can assist, and what organizational processes are required, is critical to portfolio management success. This is particularly true in the context of the rapid innovation related to portfolio management. Long term, technology and organizational process must match. Yet there are situations where technology can serve as the catalyst for organizational process improvement.

A key area for improvement is proposal submission. Project ideas, often called *project proposals*, within organizations are frequently ad hoc and lack formality. Lack of a well-thought-out process will reduce the number of proposals, or inputs, into the portfolio selection process. As with most processes, reducing the number of inputs can reduce the quality of the outputs. Having a limited list of ideas hampers any project portfolio. In the extreme, if the number of ideas you have matches the number of projects you can complete, then the portfolio selection process is obsolete. Without a list of ideas larger than you can do, you cannot make trade-offs between ideas. You would just implement all ideas, and the quality of the portfolio will suffer.

There is no shortage of innovative talent within the organization. The challenge is to harness this talent effectively. It is efficient to harness this asset, which organizations already have but are not fully using. Harnessing innovative ideas is challenging, but, if done well, it can be a rewarding part of everyone's job.

A robust portfolio selection process is a valuable component of this process. In order to achieve this, projects must be aligned with the strategic goals of the business. Ad hoc selection processes will not yield the best outcome and will not manage resources effectively. Making critical changes to portfolio selection ensures that all projects target results consistent with the organization's strategic direction.

The power of technology can support the project and portfolio management process. Communication is key and has multiple benefits, including avoiding duplication of effort, better knowledge sharing, and faster decision making and information dissemination. Workflow can underpin project processes and reduce overhead. Workflow can also help spread and entrench best practices within an organization. Technology can drive transparency across the portfolio process. The importance of a transparent organization goes beyond portfolio management. Transparency can drive broad acceptance of the portfolio management process. Ultimately, portfolio management software with proper training, adoption, and facilitation offers many opportunities for an organization to become more productive by focusing on the right objectives and executing them well.

The online resource associated with this book is www.strategic-ppm.com, which contains further detail on many of the topics discussed.

CHAPTER 1

Obtaining the Best Ideas

Innovation is the central issue in economic prosperity.
Michael Porter

THE COST OF WASTED IDEAS

In any organization, every employee possesses a unique viewpoint. These viewpoints create a tremendous opportunity. Under Toyota's production system, which is seen as world class, not utilizing these employee ideas is actually seen as a form of waste (Ohno, 1988). This waste is placed in the same category as using more raw materials than are required, or the inefficiency of having to repeat a process due to a poor quality outcome. Thinking of failure to act on employee ideas as a form of waste helps to define the opportunity for more effective portfolio management.

Employees have many ideas for improvement of the work that impacts them. Some of these may be raised in the form of questions to the manager. Why do we do it this way? Some may occur over lunch, in

1

hallway conversations, or while the employee is performing routine tasks. Many of these improvements can be made by employees on their own without the need for additional resources. Some of these ideas might entail 20 minutes of work to implement; some might require a 20-year effort. Some ideas might not merit any action when compared with other business options that meet the same need.

Although there is clearly no shortage of ideas within an organization, unfortunately, these ideas are seldom captured in most organizations, except in the few cases where a handful of employees are sufficiently entrepreneurial to drive their own ideas through to implementation. This can happen in spite of the organization, rather than because of it. Organizations are effective at focusing employees on their daily tasks, roles, and responsibilities. Organizations are far less effective at capturing the other output of that process: the ideas and observations that result from it. It is important to remember that these ideas can be more valuable than an employee's routine work. Putting in an effective process for capturing ideas provides an opportunity for organizations to leverage a resource they already have, already pay for, but fail to capture the full benefit of—namely, employee creativity.

To assume that the best ideas will somehow rise to the top, without formal means to capture them in the first place, is too optimistic. Figure 1.1 identifies the risks of such a process. This Darwinian view of the process, or of organizations, may work for a subset of ideas, but many of the ideas lost along the way have significant merit and do not get implemented for other reasons, primarily because the junior employee has no easy way to communicate an idea to the broader organization. Also, to borrow another idea from the natural sciences, rejected project ideas may be useful in the future as the starting point for new and innovative project ideas. If they are not captured, this cross-pollinating between different ideas cannot occur. Organizations must drive innovation to remain competitive, yet they often fail to take advantage of the resources they have to make that happen.

Historically, capturing, ranking, and processing these ideas in a simple way across a broad network of employees would have been a major undertaking. But today with simple, portal-based solutions combined

Manager doesn't know what to do with proposal

Next steps for implementation aren't clear

Employee can't estimate budget requirement

Employee can't communicate idea to the right people

EMPLOYEE CREATES A PROPOSAL

Employee has no way to group proposal with other similar ideas

Proposal is too late for current budget cycle and not archived

Proposal not presented in the required format

Employee doesn't know what to do with proposal

FIGURE 1.1   Risks of Informal Idea Capture Processes

with portfolio management tools, setting up a process for doing this is low-effort and low-cost. Yet, the results are dramatic.

PROJECTS AND INNOVATION

Innovation is a high priority for most organizations looking to differentiate themselves from the competition. For many organizations, sustainable organic growth is the strategic Holy Grail. Yet organizations frequently achieve far greater success with incremental improvements than innovations and consistently lament their ability to innovate. This should not be a surprise because genuine innovation is much harder to deliver consistently than incremental improvements. For example, in the field of electricity, it is easier to improve the efficiency of a steam turbine incrementally than to develop radically new, less-carbon-intensive energy sources. It is easier to make a better scalpel than it is to develop keyhole surgery. Generally, innovation requires forecasting or shaping of future trends, which is notoriously difficult, often because a combination of different trends must come together to make the idea viable. It also requires changes in organizational alignment that differ from the current organizational structure. Today's product may be contained in a single division of the organization; tomorrow's product may require multiple divisions to work together on different aspects of an innovation, while at the same time working on something that potentially threatens in-market products.

Innovation requires taking significant risk, fostering a creative mindset, and collaborating across organizational boundaries. None of which is simple to do. In combination, these challenges appear daunting. Indeed, true innovation is likely to be proceeded by many apparent failures (Farson, 1970). Conventional project management systems must share some of the blame for the lack of innovation. Application of consistent metrics across all projects may hamper innovative activity. Innovations will fail far more often than typical improvement projects. Indeed, for innovations, a 10 percent success rate is good and 20 percent is spectacular. Success rates of 20 percent or less would be viewed as a disaster for any project portfolio targeted at incremental improvement. To drive real innovation, more ideas must be captured, ideas must be allowed to feed off each other to create more ideas, and metrics for success must be relatively soft during the early stage of the process.

WHY A LONG LIST OF PROPOSALS IS NECESSARY

Many organizations I speak with have a list of projects only about as long as they can execute. This makes it almost impossible for that portfolio to be strategic. "The essence of strategy is choosing what not to do" (Porter, 2008). If your list of projects is about as long as you can execute, then clearly there is not much you're not doing. Of course, those organizations with a meager list of proposals might argue that there are many ideas that do not become proposals because they run into one impediment or another along the way. That may be true, but that sort of informal process is far from robust portfolio selection. Impediments are quite different from well-thought-out decisions. Putting in place a simple but consistent mechanism for idea capture can help dramatically increase the number of ideas that could become projects within the portfolio and magnify the portfolio's effectiveness.

Regardless of the differing levels of rigor applied to projects, if there are only a handful of formal proposals, then any idea that is given serious consideration by management is implemented. There may be some modifications to the proposal based on feedback but, nonetheless, most submitted proposals will be implemented. Sometimes, the idea list might be only slightly longer than can be executed, but this deficit might only be realized several months into portfolio execution. This is costly because even though some level of selection is occurring, there is a clear cost of starting projects only to quickly replace them when a better idea comes along.

THE RISK OF INFORMAL PROCESSES

Informal processes risk generating inconsistent outcomes. Sometimes proposals are written up and analyzed in excessive detail. Yet, in other situations, only a cursory analysis is done before committing a major investment of resources. It is also frustrating to those submitting the proposals if there is no transparency or consistent rationale as to why their projects are not selected. Without feedback, it is hard for participants to improve their proposals or even remain engaged in the process. Another problem is that sometimes the level of influence of the project champion can be more important than the quality of the project proposal itself.

A simple, transparent process is important because, in order to collect a large number of strong proposals, idea submission must be encouraged by building faith in the proposal system. Without it, there will be a reluctance to submit proposals in the first place. Greater formalization of the process can also be encouraged by including an element of employee compensation. There is an opportunity to tie employee compensation to successful proposals, whether through patent filings or a portion of the cost savings generated. Such compensation will encourage submission.

Without grouping proposals together and analyzing them, it is a leap of faith to believe that the organization has naturally developed a process to get the best ideas onto the table without anyone consciously taking any explicit action or making any decision at the aggregate level. The ad hoc process is likely to be inefficient and more time consuming than a more structured portfolio selection process. Portfolio selection offers the opportunity to analyze proposals en masse, which can make it easier to calibrate across the group and can create efficiencies through economies of scale.

To take an extreme example, batch prioritization might require one meeting for 100 projects, as opposed to 100 ad hoc meetings if each project were considered individually. Therefore, it is key not just to have more ideas but to group those ideas together to ensure meaningful prioritization that is efficient from a time-management perspective. The grouping together of ideas is also helpful because it provides the opportunity to group similar proposals together into larger, richer proposals, and for the combination of proposals to spur new thinking and proposals. If proposals are considered in smaller sets—or worse, on an ad hoc basis as each proposal comes in—much of this cross-fertilization may not occur and an opportunity for further innovation is lost.

Another level of rigor can be applied to particularly risky or critically important projects. Here, proposals can be held in reserve to be executed, should the primary project fail or go irretrievably off course—as will likely occur across a large portfolio. For example, new problems may arise that need addressing, or compelling new ideas may arise based on customer feedback or market and competitive analysis. Although these ideas are healthy and often superior to project proposals being executed, this can disrupt the process, since the attempt to configure the portfolio on the fly is unlikely to lead to an optimal outcome. Resources on a canceled project will have been wasted, and recalibrating the project portfolio too frequently as new ideas come up may not be an effective use of time and resources. Managing this balance is critical; altering the portfolio creates adjustment costs, but reacting to changing market conditions rapidly and effectively can differentiate an organization from its competition.

It is rare that organizations are able to develop a broad and extensive list of projects to truly prioritize explicitly. Nonetheless, it is a complete list that enables strategic alignment in project selection. Without an extensive list of options, how can you arrive at the best permutation? As Napoleon said, "To govern is to choose." But how can you choose without options? The best ideas do not come from you. The best ideas emerge from within your organization, given the unique perspectives of the different divisions and functional roles. These ideas must then be consistently reviewed so that you can meaningfully rank them against each other. It is clear that any attempt to prioritize ideas must start with an effective mechanism for capturing a large number of potential project ideas. This must occur even before the formal project proposal stage.

LOWERING THE BAR FOR IDEA SUBMISSION

The main reason for a lack of good project ideas within most organizations is simply that it is hard for employees to know what to do with their ideas. Ideas are not asked for explicitly from a broad enough set of people, in a transparent enough fashion, and on a regular enough basis. Idea generation typically is something that is seen as being valuable, but until recently, the technology has not been available for broad and simple idea capture, and the significant implementation costs have made most organizations reluctant to explore the area. Executives are receptive to new project ideas and would like to hear more of them—especially within a streamlined, simple process—but often the process for submitting project ideas is too complex or, worse, not defined. If all ideas must be justified by a 20-page analytical report listing the expected financial benefits and strategic rationale, then the number of ideas submitted will be low and, indeed, very similar to the set of ideas management already sees.

Often, the person able to come up with the spark of a new idea may not have the skills to perform a full analysis to justify or flesh it out in rigorous fashion. However, others must do that analysis in order to ensure that the best ideas are executed, or at least reach the stage where that analysis can be done. Therefore, more important than having a process is making sure that the process is simple and available to all within the organization.

Case Study: Managing a New Product Portfolio

Scott is managing a portfolio of new product launches. The goal is to extend an existing international consumer products company into new geographies and markets. Scott is "aiming toward incrementality" and "trying to be very efficient with his spend." As there are many existing competitors in the market, there are a lot of analogs to existing products that could be introduced, Scott says, "We could not invent for 5 years and still bring out new product." However, Scott takes a "core-satellite" approach to the portfolio, first targeting higher-volume products to lead well in new markets and build relationships with partners, and then focusing on innovation, particularly in markets where innovation is expected by consumers such as Japan.

Scott's process is fairly dynamic, built around monthly reviews with core stakeholders and quarterly reviews with all the international partner teams. In addition, the CEO will periodically contribute ideas into the pipeline based on market and competitive observations so the set of ideas under consideration is constantly expanding. It is easy to introduce a feasibility study for any product, but the amount of effort required to build the full business case, including financial estimates, can vary depending on how established the category is. As such, business cases are living documents. Testing is conducted to minimize risk. Concepts are tested online or via focus groups to generate more information that can feed into financial assessments. However, there is no mandated process for testing; the overall goal is to reduce financial risk through reducing uncertainty. "I don't mind some uncertainty if the finance stakes are low," he says. In cases where financial estimates are more uncertain, more testing will be performed; in areas where financial uncertainty is less, testing phases will be skipped to lower cost and increase speed to market.

Projects are ranked systematically across four core criteria:

1. Supply chain issues (cost, manufacturing feasibility, shelf life, etc.)
2. Market opportunity (customer demand, value proposition, incrementality)
3. Brand (degree of alignment with brand positioning)
4. Compete (competitive threats and responses)

The resulting rankings are fairly "fluid" as new information comes in; for products that are not in development, ranking is less of an issue. But for the top six or so products in the active pipeline, reprioritization is common and encouraged as new information is learned from test results and feasibility studies, though products are typically only "knocked out completely for manufacturing or distribution reasons." Some products are also unlikely to ever be in development because of brand "guard rails" that make the company unlikely to invest in areas that are inconsistent with what their brand represents. Priorities may also change based on distribution deals with new markets, since "Japan, Korea, and the UK are all different" if we decide to enter a certain market, that may change our development priorities. Also, in development if we "spend a couple of months and can't get where we need to be," that product will also likely be reprioritized.

USING SIMPLE IDEA CAPTURE

Providing a simplified, streamlined process for idea submission can increase project proposals and result in a better portfolio of projects. Simplification is not about reducing the quality of ideas, but about reducing the bureaucracy associated with producing them. Simplification is not easy, as it involves defining what is really needed before further due diligence is conducted on the project. It also means making the submission process easy to follow and locate and driving awareness of it. In terms of a simplified proposal, a relatively brief description with broad estimates of key parameters, such as budget and headcount, is all that is needed. In fact, sometimes all that is needed is the idea, and the budgetary angle can be left until later in the process. Then as the

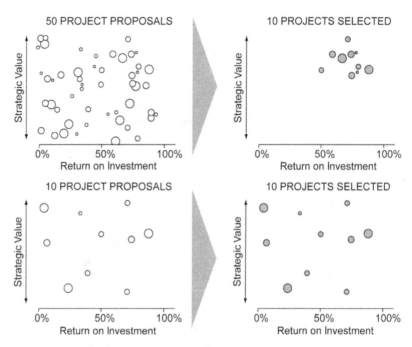

FIGURE 1.2   Benefit of More Project Proposals

proposal moves through the process and gets closer to implementation, more detail can be added—perhaps by introducing a step to develop a detailed business case into the process, assuming the idea is selected at an initial stage. In this way, no proposal is more detailed than it needs to be. In addition, less effort is wasted on filling out what might be superfluous information because the proposal may not make it that far during the selection process.

Having this process in place helps maximize the number of ideas, which must be the central goal of the idea submission process in order for it to succeed. Figure 1.2 shows how having more ideas to choose from can lead to a superior portfolio of projects being selected. During this stage, it can be helpful to focus more on the benefits than the costs or impediments. It is likely that the organization is more aware of the costs and pitfalls of particular actions than of the benefits of moving into an unexplored area. Therefore, proposals should center on a clear description of the idea and potential benefits, and then the cost estimates can come later, should the potential benefits of the project warrant it. The key is that less time spent on a submission process means that less time is invested in each idea, and so more ideas are forthcoming. A side benefit of this lightweight approach is that an idea that has not been fully polished is less likely to become a pet project of anyone before it gets approved, and a simplified submission process makes it easier to reject ideas, without the problem of investing too much in concepts that will never see implementation. This can be important because the more that can be done to make the process objective and transparent, the more interest and excitement will be built around it.

A more democratic idea submission process creates the opportunity for less-senior employees to submit ideas. This group of employees has a wealth of knowledge about particular parts of the organization that executives may have little exposure to. Therefore, a more democratic—and simply easier—process for idea submission is likely to lead not only to more ideas but also to broader ideas. The ultimate result is a better portfolio because the range of possible projects is significantly expanded.

THE VALUE OF RANGE-BASED ESTIMATION

Another benefit of a simplified project proposal process is that contributors are not locked into specific but inaccurate estimates at an early stage. Keeping estimates range-based makes it more likely that estimates can converge toward their true value as more data are obtained. If a point estimate must be provided early in the process, it is less likely to converge on the true value. This is partly due to the psychological effect of *anchoring* (i.e., when an estimate that is introduced into the process gains some credibility), regardless of the accuracy of the underlying assumptions, and the estimate is then less likely to move than if no estimate existed. Having no estimate whatsoever poses its own problems, so using a range-based estimation process is the best approach; the issue of anchoring doesn't disappear but it is less acute with a range rather than a point estimate. Figure 1.3 shows how the margin of error for a particular project cost estimate reduces over time as the project gets closer to implementation.

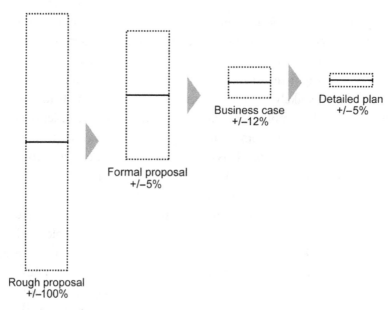

FIGURE 1.3   Range-Based Estimation

ANCHORING

The impact of anchoring was identified by Tversky and Kahneman in a 1974 article. Their key insight was that estimation processes "are biased toward the initial values" regardless of whether those initial values make any real sense; this is believed to be because insufficient adjustment occurs from those values. For example, in estimating percentages, such as the percentage of African countries in the United Nations, when people were asked, "Is the percentage of African countries in the UN higher or lower than 10 percent?" they ultimately estimated 25 percent when asked what the actual percentage was. Surprisingly, those who were asked "Is the percentage of African countries in the UN higher or lower than 65 percent?" estimated that the actual percentage was 45 percent. Thus, a higher initial estimate, even if the participants knew it was randomly determined, caused estimates to change materially.

It might be argued that portfolio management is a serious business so this problem will not occur, but Tversky and Kahneman found that offering payoffs for people to be more accurate did not improve accuracy, and the impact of the random first estimate remained powerful. These results are persuasive and suggest that in project management, the initial estimate you come to, even if it is determined in a very basic manner, even randomly, has a powerful impact on future estimates due to insufficient adjustment from this starting value. This means that the initial estimate should be delayed if at all possible, or given as a broad range, and the problem of insufficient adjustment should be given real attention by management to ensure that estimates of key factors such as the portfolio budget really do evolve over time to reflect true values.

Source: Amos Tversky and Daniel Kahneman, "Judgment under Uncertainty: Heuristics and Biases by Science," *New Series,* vol. 185 (4157), (September 27, 1974): 1124–1131.

GENERATING EXCITEMENT

A robust idea submission process has limited value without broad awareness of the process across the organization. A crucial aspect of any process is driving interest and excitement around it. It is important that employees are made aware of the process and want to contribute. Awareness should be raised in innovative ways, perhaps by highlighting those ideas that are noteworthy. Another incentive can be demonstrating the success and impact of ideas that come from people outside of the traditional portfolio decision team. Generating enthusiasm and excitement around the submission process is critical to drive more ideas through the system, further improving the output of the whole process. Once again, the more that can be done to build broad participation in the process, the better the outcomes that the process will achieve. To implement a diverse set of projects, which is often helpful from a risk management perspective, a diverse set of ideas is valuable.

Another way to generate excitement is to enable participants to not just submit ideas but to also participate in a preliminary ranking process, assigning a start ranking to proposals according to their perceived merit. This technique is sometimes referred to as *crowd sourcing*, which can be valuable in situations where a large number of ideas are submitted. Here, a very simple peer review process can serve as a simple preliminary filter for ideas. For example, only ideas receiving a certain rating receive formal consideration. Collaborative ranking of ideas also builds engagement in the process; since all ideas are transparent, participants may devise their own project proposals in the process of ranking others. In addition, through rating the ideas of others, the enthusiasm and interest in the portfolio selection process will increase.

Another option for process engagement is to tie successful submissions to the firm's incentive structure. In this way, employees can be financially rewarded if their proposals and ideas are implemented. Incentives might be provided for a particular subset of ideas. For example, employees might receive a bonus if their ideas result in a patent filing. Incentives can be tied to ideas that result in successful project *outcomes* in order to reduce the incentive of just submitting ideas, which would put the emphasis on submitting ideas that might have a high chance of business impact. Using this approach depends on the corporate culture; it can boost idea submissions, but it might also make employees less willing to work collaboratively on proposals if the rewards go to the individual and not the team.

MAKING PROCESSES TRANSPARENT

Excitement can be further enhanced by a transparent process. When employees understand how the process works, they are more likely to support and contribute. Putting in place clear, transparent benchmarks improves portfolio performance. Sharing the strategic goals helps the end-to-end process of project management. It also likely means you will get better projects in the first place. If everyone knows what the target is, effort spent on projects that are futile is minimized. The process has most context, so ideas receive sufficient improvement before submission. This improves the caliber of proposals. Knowing these benchmarks ahead of time will help focus proposals on the areas the organization cares about and will ensure that the proposals are written to address the areas that matter. Transparency will help idea submission so the process is not a black box. Feedback should be provided on rejected ideas so that better proposals can be created in the future, or rejected ideas can be refined to merge into compelling suggestions for future prioritization processes. In this way, the process should improve over time as the quality of submissions is refined and the objectives of the process are clear. Providing feedback on rejected proposals is an important way to improve idea submission over time, so that the overall quality of ideas will improve.

Making the process transparent also helps with process improvement. If all participants understand the process, then they are better able to suggest improvements to it. In this way, creating transparency is valuable not just for increasing engagement with the process but for the improvement of the process itself.

MAKING PROCESSES SIMPLE

Simplicity is the key to collecting the largest number of ideas from the broadest set of participants. Transparency and excitement will go a long way to driving engagement among your employees, but a simple capture process will increase the number of ideas you are able to receive as various blocking issues are removed. It makes it easy for those who want to engage in the process to do so. The challenge is understanding what you really need to collect. Every move to simplify the process involves potentially removing a valuable piece of data. Early on, it may not be clear what data are essential to capture, resulting in more data being collected than are ultimately needed due to this uncertainty. This is difficult to overcome in the short term, but as soon as the process is established, you can monitor which data are necessary for decision making and cut everything that is not. Without constantly reducing the reporting burden, the process will inevitably become bureaucratic over time. Bureaucratic processes are not conducive to transparency and excitement, and can lead to the demise of the process.

It is important to remember that at the first stage of the process, the only data necessary to capture are what enable an informed decision to be made on whether an idea should reach the second stage. Thinking about data capture in those terms can help with process refinement and maximize idea submission.

USING SUPERIOR ESTIMATION

The barriers to submitting an idea should be low, but they should offer sufficient structure to be useful. Setting *confidence bands* is an appropriate way to enable this. A confidence band gives a high and a low estimate for a particular value. For example, for the total financial cost of a project, the very early estimate of cost might be given as $1 million to $3 million. This is, of course, a very wide range, but it gives some indication of where the cost might lie without wasting effort on a detailed forecasting process before it is known whether the project will proceed. Then as the project is formally assessed, the range might narrow to $1.25 million to $2.25 million after preliminary estimation is complete, and then at the approval stage, the range is $1.75 million to $2 million, and then at formal project launch after a detailed budget is constructed, the cost is $1,815,000. This method avoids wasted effort on forecasting and does not lock down the budget before all the details of the project are formally defined. This is very important because inaccurate cost estimates are often not due to inaccurately costing out the work involved but, rather, from not capturing the entire scope of work for the project. Of course, this estimate band concept can be applied not just to budgets but also to other important project attributes, such as resource utilization or the schedule itself.

The estimation process should also tie back to the goal of the proposal itself. If the project is time critical, then an elegant estimation process may actually result in project failure, and a greater margin of estimation error may be tolerable. However, if a project is centered on cost savings and efficiency from a cost management standpoint, then efficient estimation processes are likely to be more important.

GOING BEYOND THE EMPLOYEE

Just as senior executives do not have all the good ideas, neither is everyone who has a proposal for improving your organization employed by your company. Consider inviting customers, vendors, or suppliers into the idea submission process. Once again, a different perspective will yield different ideas for projects that could be executed and will help diversity across the project portfolio. Think creatively about how ideas can be captured from anyone who has a perspective on your business. Of course, in moving outside the employee base, the bar for idea submission must be even lower, and employees will have to encourage and develop the ideas that stem from those outside the organization. However, fostering these ideas is likely to provide a wealth of material for developing the organization in ways that the conventional thinking of those steeped in the traditions of the organization might not be able to see. If security procedures do not permit granting access to nonemployees, consider allowing employees to submit ideas on behalf of others and work with those outside the organization to capture ideas. Often, those outside the organization can have powerful project suggestions. Capturing ideas and proposals from customers directly is ideal and can strengthen relationships beyond simply executing on the project in question.

MANAGING PROJECTS ACROSS THE SUPPLY CHAIN

Further consideration of broadening the scope of idea submission also leads to consideration of broadening the scope of project execution to include projects that involve working with customers or across the supply chain. Of course, this is a natural outcome of the process and should be encouraged. It is unlikely that the best projects are completely within the scope of the organization to implement, and though these broader projects will be more challenging to implement, the benefits of doing so will also be greater. Developments in technology now make it easy to manage projects beyond the boundaries of the enterprise on a single system, and your projects should have the same scope as your business. Running a hosted project management system can enable access from different organizations on an equal footing.

WHERE ARE YOUR IDEAS COMING FROM?

The way to get good ideas is to get lots of ideas and throw the bad ones away.
Linus Pauling

Where are you getting your ideas from? Executives in an organization do not have all the good ideas. Do you have a process for employees to submit ideas for consideration? What about customers or other businesses that partner with you or form part of your supply chain? Are you leveraging their ideas and expertise? Typically, lengthening the list of project ideas can also increase the quality of ideas. It is likely that the first few projects that come to mind are the work that must get done—the operational imperatives for the organization or a repeat of work that was done last year. That is important, but there are many other ideas you are missing. It is only by broadening the number of ideas you consider that you will get away from a run-of-the-mill project portfolio to one that is truly strategic in its impact and includes innovative ideas that will really drive your business forward and differentiate you from your competitors.

Batch versus Ad Hoc Prioritization

It is important that ideas are compared against each other. Any reasonable project has merit in isolation; it is only by comparing projects and associated resources that an effective conclusion on which proposals to implement can be reached. For example, if two projects require the same strategic resource at the same time, only one can proceed. Beyond resource constraints, there is the need to manage the project portfolio in the way any financial portfolio should be managed. Key considerations include managing risk. Risk should be balanced across the portfolio, and risk should be diversified so that all projects are exposed to different risks. Breadth of objectives is also important; if every project is a cost-cutting project, then that has an impact on business performance and revenue growth will be reduced. It is only by treating projects as a portfolio that these trade-offs can be managed effectively.

Faster Starts versus Robust Prioritization

Typically, organizations start projects as needed. The idea of delaying a critical project is not acceptable given business imperatives, and so the project starts straight away. In some cases, this is the only possible course of action; in others, a batch process for project selection makes more sense. A batch process is one where potential projects or project proposals are grouped together to be prioritized so that of, for example, 50 potential projects, the top 30 can be implemented. The advantage of batch selection is that trade-offs can be made to create the most effective portfolio of projects.

If projects are considered on a more ad hoc basis as they come in, then the optimal portfolio cannot be achieved without potentially stopping in-flight projects, which is a waste of resources. To be clear, there is nothing wrong with stopping a project if it is not meeting its targets or if circumstances have changed, but cutting a project simply because your selection process wasn't sophisticated enough to consider all relevant proposals suggests a need for process improvement. A further benefit of batch selection is efficient usage of executives' time because to be effective, the prioritization discussion involves a meeting of several executives. It also works better with context—all prioritization is relative, so choosing between projects simultaneously is likely to achieve a better result than choosing projects in series.

Therefore, there is a trade-off between running a batch prioritization relative to prioritizing project ideas as they come in. A *batch process* is more efficient in terms of reaching an optimal portfolio and reducing time spent on the process. On-the-fly prioritization is most commonly used and minimizes delay for any given project, but it also implies constant churn within the portfolio. In practice, prioritization is a continuum rather than an either-or decision, and the question is how often prioritization should happen. Annual or quarterly prioritization processes tend to manage this trade-off most effectively, but the exact frequency should be less often if the cost of doing the prioritization work is high and should be more often if the cost of delaying projects is high.

KEY QUESTIONS

- How are you splitting your metrics and processes for innovative and traditional projects?
- Are your expectations for innovative projects distinct from those related to process improvement?

- How many ideas are you really considering on your project shortlist?
- How can you increase the ratio of ideas to executed projects?
- Can you lower the barrier of ideas to submission? Can you widen the net of people who can submit ideas?
- Can you make the process more transparent and less bureaucratic?
- Do you really use everything required in a project proposal to make a go/no-go decision on a project?
- What are you consciously choosing not to do? How is that decision being made?
- Are you comparing projects against each other, or just dealing with issues as they come up?

SUGGESTED READINGS

For more detail on the innovative production methods pioneered by Toyota, see Taiichi Ohno, *Toyota Production System: Beyond Large-Scale Production* (Productivity Press, 1998).

For a more on innovation, see Richard Farson, *The Innovation Paradox: The Success of Failure, the Failure of Success* (The Free Press, 1970).

Michael Porter's thoughts on strategy are discussed in more detail in Michael Porter, *On Strategy* (Harvard Business Press, 2008).

The problem of anchoring is discussed in more detail in Amos Tversky and Daniel Kahneman, "Judgment under Uncertainty: Heuristics and Biases by Science," *New Series*, vol. 185 (4157), (September 27, 1974): 1124–1131.

For an interesting discussion of decision-making and analysis by project managers, see Kishore Sengupta, Tarek K. Adbel-Hamid, and Luk N. Van Wassenhove, "The Experience Trap," *Harvard Business Review* (February 2008).

For a rich and accessible discussion of how decisions are made and can be improved in a host of situations, see Richard H. Thaler and Cass R. Sunstein, *Nudge: Improving Decisions About Health, Wealth, and Happiness* (New Haven, CT: Yale University Press, 2008).

For a discussion of the difference between strategic planning and strategic thinking, see Henry Mintzberg, "The Rise and Fall of Strategic Planning," *Harvard Business Review* (January 1994).

For further updates and information on the topics discussed on this chapter, see www.strategicppm.com.

CHAPTER 2

Selecting Impactful Projects

Management is doing things right; leadership is doing the right things.
Peter Drucker

ALIGNING PROJECTS AND STRATEGY

Many organizations have a well-defined and well-scoped strategic process. This can be augmented by better and broader idea capture to provide supportive tactics, but execution is the critical challenge. Indeed, as is widely recognized, weakness in execution, not weakness in strategy, is a primary reason for CEO failure. Knowing this, it is important to tie the strategic theory governing the business to the experience of project management. Without this linkage, either the project portfolio is blind to the needs of the business or the strategic goals are empty, with no support at the execution level. It is clear that this is an area that businesses must get right for long-term success.

21

REASON FOR CEO FAILURE

There is much evidence that CEO failure is driven not by poor strategy but by poor execution. A *Fortune* magazine study of several dozen CEOs in 1999 suggested that 70 percent of CEOs who failed did so because of poor execution: "It is bad execution. As simple as that." A study of 200 companies in the United Kingdom found similar results: 80 percent of company directors felt that they had the right strategy, but only 14 percent felt that those strategies were being implemented well. In 2005, Michael Mankins of Marakon Associates, after conducting research in conjunction with the *Economist's* Intelligence Unit, also identified execution as the major problem, stating, "Less than 15 percent of companies routinely track how they perform over how they thought they were going to perform." It appears that though the challenges in creating an effective strategy should not be understated, it is in effectively executing on those strategies that companies fall down, often due to lack of follow-up and tracking. If the strategy is abstract, executing against it will be a challenge. If the strategy is translated into actionable project goals, success becomes within reach and progress toward attaining success is measurable.

Source: R. Charan and G. Colvin, "Why CEOs Fail," *Fortune* (June 21, 1999).

Putting Strategy First

Strategy needs to come before portfolio selection. In order to select the right set of projects, the *strategic goals* must be defined in advance. Furthermore, the strategic goals should ideally be relatively limited: three to seven goals are best so that projects can be consistently benchmarked across all of the strategic goals, and the effort of doing this is not overwhelming. It helps to think of it as a matrix, with 50 proposals and 7 strategic goals, creating 350 mappings between projects and goals that must take place. With 20 goals, the number of mappings required would be 1,000. This is not the only reason to keep the number of strategic goals low, but it is a relevant factor.

Having a small number of goals also helps to keep the goals memorable and at the necessary high level, thus avoiding strategic goals blurring with the tactics from their implementation. Of course, the process of linking projects to strategic goals is critical. If the projects you undertake don't reflect your strategy, then what does? It is much less likely that operational work has a strategic impact relative to projects, which are more likely to create some level of change within the organization.

This process also entails that the strategic goals are reasonably broad—the sort of goals that are likely to remain valid for the next three years or longer, rather than the next three months. The duration of your strategic goals should be at least as long as time required to implement projects and realize the benefits from the projects that support them. If strategic goals are narrowly defined and numerous, then they are unlikely to be applicable to a broad portfolio of projects. It is also important that the strategy is at the same *altitude* as the portfolio of projects being analyzed. If the projects are from across the business, then the strategy, too, should apply to the entire business; but if the projects are just a subset of all projects, such as only IT projects, then prioritizing them against IT's strategic goals makes the most sense. The correct way to perform the prioritization is to have the projects and strategic goals defined at the same level.

Though the strategic goal definition must come before project selection, it must not be rushed. Selecting the right strategy is imperative for running an impactful portfolio. A poor strategy executed flawlessly is still a failure. It is important to take the time to refine your strategic plan to ensure that it effectively explores all the options for your business and leads to a well-reasoned, robust portfolio outcome.

Definition of strategic goals is likely to be time consuming, as it is the outcome of an extensive strategic planning process and will require the building of consensus across senior executives throughout the business. Creating this consensus will require time and commitment from the executives involved in the process. The strategic goal-setting process is broader than the management of the project portfolio, but it is a necessary prerequisite for the portfolio selection process. It is worth investing considerable time in this process to achieve this important result—it sets up the other stages of the process for success. Also, though understanding strategic goals is vital for success, since it can be a time-consuming process, it is also important to be comfortable with a more informal process while the goals are being defined so as not to delay ongoing work.

The Importance of SMART Goals

These strategic goals must be clear. Ambiguity at this stage leads to ambiguity in execution. Using SMART goals will aid you in communicating your strategy. Do not allow disagreement between senior leadership to result in a vague strategy. Confront the areas of disagreement rather than settling for vague goals.

Setting SMART goals is an effective way of focusing the strategy of the project. Each goal should have the following characteristics:

- *Specific.* Very clear description of what the goal is. For example, reduce packaging input costs at the Toledo plant.
- *Measurable.* A measurable definition of success. For example, packaging cost is a useful example, as it can be measured in dollars. However, if there is any ambiguity about the accounting standards to be used, that should be specified.
- *Actionable.* The goal is something the individual or organization can influence. For example, if the cost were to reflect only commodity price pass-through that the organization cannot change, the goal is not actionable.
- *Results-focused.* Oriented toward outcomes or results. In our example, reducing expenditure and thereby increasing profit would be a results-focused goal.
- *Time-bound.* Have a clear deadline or time for completion. For example, in this case, the cost-benefit analysis could be targeted for the third quarter of the financial year.

CREATING PORTFOLIO ALIGNMENT

Once strategic goals have been defined, which is itself a nontrivial process, mapping them to projects is relatively straightforward. Each project can be examined to see the extent to which it supports each of the strategic goals and an overall prioritization of projects achieved. This is a key step in the prioritization process. The goal is not to choose the 10 projects with the highest return on investment, but to ensure that the projects map to the strategic goals of the business. This process is the first step in aligning the projects with the strategic goals of the business and, ultimately, determining the extent to which each project will advance the strategy.

Mapping Projects to Strategy

Each project can be mapped to each business strategy, to the extent that each project supports that strategy. It is unlikely that any particular project supports all the strategies of the business. If strategies are sufficiently broad, then it is unlikely that one project can cover them all, and even these projects may not be optimal from a cost or resource perspective. Identifying the one or two super projects is not the goal of the process, since they are probably readily apparent anyway. The value is primarily in the projects that support one or two goals strongly, a few others to different degrees, and others not at all. It is likely that a large number of projects are in this category. It is here that you get the most benefit from taking a portfolio approach. Virtually all projects offer strategic value, but in selecting some and not others on an ad hoc basis, it is hard to see the overall composition of the portfolio and harder still to optimize it to find the most efficient option. By using a strategic mapping process, it is quite possible to see, for any subset of projects selected, which strategic areas are being invested in and which are being neglected. Without portfolio selection algorithms, that analysis is hard for anyone to perform manually, especially for a large portfolio where "what-if" analyses are needed to iterate to get to the best portfolio. This is an area where as the number of data points increases, so algorithms increasingly perform better than humans in presenting optimized sets of projects to meet a particular set of goals.

Figure 2.1 shows what strategic alignment means. The dark gray bars show management's analysis of the relative weighting of strategic goals. Increasing the rate of innovation is the most important goal, whereas reducing working capital is relatively less important. However, the light gray bars show where portfolio resources are being allocated, and there it is clear that too little is being invested on projects that increase the

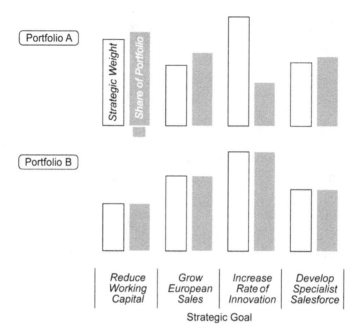

FIGURE 2.1   Portfolio Alignment

rate of innovation, because too much is being invested in the other areas. Portfolio B shows an example where the strategic goals and the allocation of portfolio resources are well aligned.

There is also the opportunity to make this process iterative. Some proposals may be too broad in scope, and focusing them directly on a single strategic goal might be desirable to fill a strategic gap within the portfolio. Equally, other ideas may not be broad enough, given particular needs. Just as the mapping process provides insight on the best projects to implement, it might also offer an opportunity to think about the best projects to refine in order to improve their strategic impact and chance of selection to the portfolio.

One Portfolio or Many?

Projects targeted at innovation and those at improvement should be managed separately. This is because metrics for success and expectations of success are quite different. Furthermore, the timing of returns on innovation will differ. An innovative project might yield nothing for the first five years but dramatic growth thereafter; whereas a maintenance project might yield a steady single-digit return. Managing innovative and process improvement projects in the same manner is likely to lead to mismanagement of either the innovative or the incremental projects, and most likely it is the innovative projects that will be curtailed. In the worst case, grouping together different types of projects could even cause both to be mismanaged. This is because the management style necessary for innovative projects is significantly different from that required of a maintenance project portfolio. For a conventional project portfolio, the power of management rests primarily in the veto. For innovation, the goal of management is to coalesce ideas into workable solutions.

Therefore, although it can seem efficient to have a single project portfolio—and indeed, there are advantages to doing so for optimization—in practice, it is important that innovative and improvement projects are not managed in the same fashion, given the unique needs of each.

In practice, this means there is one overall portfolio to monitor where resources are allocated but differing treatment of innovative projects versus improvement projects. This might mean using different workflow and selection criteria, depending on the project in question.

The Benefits of Strategic Alignment

Achieving strategic alignment should result in greater strategic bang for the buck—more strategic execution for the same project budget, or greater efficiency—achieving the same level of strategic results for less resources. Either way, organizations can be sure that they are on the efficient frontier and achieve the maximum return for the level of resources committed to the portfolio.

Creating the portfolio through a process of strategic alignment makes different analyses or pivots on the data possible. The incremental return at each level of spending is evident, and rather than setting a budget based on last year's spending level, it is possible to see what the optimal budget is based on the return profile of the project portfolio. Budgets can grow and shrink based on the strategic possibilities available to the business in a given fiscal year or quarter and across different groups or divisions of the organization. This is more efficient than the typical rule of thumb of last year's budget plus or minus a certain percentage. Adopting a portfolio process to managing the budget also means that dollars can be allocated against forecasted results, and allocations in future years can be linked to delivery against those goals. Making this process transparent will help the understanding of the portfolio management process and make the bar clear for the returns necessary for a project to attract funding. It is also important to combine this with a clear process of risk management, and it is important that the benefit of superior returns is not matched with an unwelcome increase in risk across the portfolio.

Case Study: Creating Alignment in Pharmaceuticals

Marc Gawley optimizes project portfolios for pharmaceutical clients in Europe and Asia, particularly in the course of merger integrations. The key objective, perhaps counterintuitively, is not to invest in the best drugs in terms of individual revenue but to ensure that the resulting portfolio is balanced and focused on the key therapeutic areas of the business. The need for alignment across the portfolio is what matters for success. In the context of a merger, it may not be sensible to incorporate all the blockbuster brands of both parties. Some may not have sufficient sales within the physician segments that the new organization will focus on, whereas others may be difficult for a single sales force to reconcile and promote given earlier "combative" positioning. The key objective is to have a broad set of areas covered in line with the strategic vision of the business and the expertise of the sales and marketing organization. This is a classic example of portfolio management, where not just the individual areas of investment but also the relationships between them determine the optimal portfolio. It is this ability to track the dynamic relationships between projects that makes portfolio management so valuable in enabling organizations to maximize their productivity.

Forcing In and Forcing Out Projects

Of course, not all portfolios are completely unconstrained to simply align to the goals of the business. Projects may have to be undertaken for legal reasons. There might be contractual commitments or some other factors that are not necessarily strategic but are binding on the organization. Some highly attractive projects may not be possible because of other constraints. Sometimes outsourcing, joint ventures, or partnerships block what would otherwise be desirable projects. Some ideas may be vetoed for internal political reasons. Although these constraints are seldom completely insurmountable, modeling the portfolio in this way can enable you to calculate the effect of either forcing in or forcing out particular projects to and from the portfolio. In this way, it is possible to assess the financial cost and strategic cost of any constraints placed on the organization, and to identify the optimal portfolio to adjust to such constraints. This analysis cannot remove the constraints in the short term, but it provides a way to assess the costs and benefits of minimizing such constraints in the future. It is sometimes easy for one executive to veto a particular project based on political power, but knowing the true cost of that decision based on the strategic impact can support optimal management of the portfolio.

GOING BEYOND STRATEGIC ALIGNMENT

A focus that is solely on strategic alignment neglects other metrics, such as return on investment, internal rate of return, payback period, and estimates of risk. These should be included in the analysis, too, especially if all the so-called strategic projects offer low financial returns. The idea of strategic alignment should be thought of as a tool. It is a particular metric within the decision process, rather than the answer. Using it in combination with other prioritization techniques is likely to yield a richer outcome than one method alone. In addition, the discussion the process generates is also likely to be just as valuable to the organization as the permutations of project options are discussed. The optimal portfolio is likely to come from a combination of more mathematical optimization of the portfolio and discussions between those within the organization who have different experiences and perspectives. Ultimately, people, rather than data, make decisions. However, a thorough analysis of the strategic alignment of the portfolio will create a good first cut of the projects for the business to implement and will start the discussion with a strong foundation. As conversations progress, what-if analyses can be done to support different sets of the projects and to examine the business impact. The goal is not to replace manual selection with a metric-driven process, but to supplement ad hoc discussion with more formal modeling of the optimal portfolio, given the strategic goals of the business. Given the complexity of the process, adding some mathematical rigor to it can be enormously beneficial.

Setting Aggressive Goals

I believe in always having goals and always setting them high.

Sam Walton

Project management processes naturally tend toward goal setting, which is important; but just as important for success is ensuring that the goal is ambitious. There are dozens of books on the topic of negotiation that emphasize the importance of bold goals for successful negotiation outcomes, and the same is true of projects. Academic research that supports the value of goal setting across organizations—for example, Terpstra and Rozell (1994)—found a significant positive relationship between goal-setting and organizational profits, based on a survey of 6,000 employees. It also makes intuitive sense; if you target something, you are far more likely to achieve it.

It is better to aim at perfection and miss than to aim at imperfection and hit it.

Thomas J. Watson

The Cultural Importance of Goal Setting

Implementing a project management system provides a means of institutionalizing goal setting within the organization and monitoring progress toward those goals in a structured and predefined way. The act of setting goals should encourage greater organizational focus and foster innovative solutions where needed in order to achieve the desired goal-based outcomes. If the implementation of the portfolio management system can drive a culture of aggressive goal setting with corresponding accountability, then the benefit will be significant. Indeed, the effects of aggressive goal setting can be so powerful that it may be one of the major contributions of the portfolio management system.

APPLYING PORTFOLIO THEORY TO PORTFOLIO SELECTION

Modern portfolio theory is a financial concept used for allocating money between investments, but it can be applied to a selection of projects within organizations. This is because the two processes are conceptually similar. It is no accident that the term *portfolio* is equally applicable to both projects and financial investments. The theory states that for any allocation of resources, there is an efficient set that yields the greatest return for a given level of risk, while the right level of resources to allocate to projects cannot be known without considering further factors. What is clear is that once that level of investment is determined, there is then an optimal set of projects to implement for a given level of risk and investment.

The theory is elegant when applied to a relatively narrow and well-defined set of asset classes, such as stocks and bonds, but the challenge is to capture sufficient data in a way that is not too onerous to make the same methodology applicable to the management of a portfolio of projects. Once this is done, one can be assured that project budgets are being effectively used in terms of financial or strategic return. Without this approach, your portfolio is likely to be wasteful, and you could either achieve more impact for the same investment, or achieve the same results with less investment. Either way, not having an efficient portfolio of projects is costly.

THE VALUE OF PRIVATE INFORMATION COLLECTION

Portfolio selection is likely to involve many different stakeholders. Reaching consensus is a time-consuming and inexact process. In these discussions, it can be helpful to collect opinions through private voting first. Using this method allows all opinions to be represented, albeit anonymously, and makes it easier to identify divergence of opinion within the group. Areas of consensus should be easy to make progress on, and a greater amount of time can be spent on the areas of disagreement. By using private collection of information, everyone is able to voice an opinion, unbiased by the opinions of others. Without collecting information privately, the first person to speak may influence the other participants to agree with them, especially if that person is senior. One caveat is that the culture of the organization should be respected, even though private collection of information often leads to better decision making. If the organization itself is very structured and hierarchical, then a democratic decision-making process, even if superior, may not be sustainable given the way decisions are made within the organization. Nonetheless, private collection of information can be a valuable part of most selection processes.

THE RISK OF COMMITMENT ESCALATION

Psychology and economics combine to make an important point to re-inforce at the project selection phase. Any money already spent on a project is gone: "Sunk costs are sunk," to use the economic expression. Rationally, that is easy to understand—in fact, it is obvious. Yet, psycho-logically, it is challenging to be conscious of the problem in your own thinking and correct for it. Many bad decisions are made with ongoing projects because the idea of reversing course and abandoning past work is hard. From a portfolio perspective, what this means is that last year's project should not receive funding just because it is already in flight. In many cases, continuation of existing projects will make sense, but only if last year's rationale still holds. Of course, markets change, progress doesn't always match plan, and the portfolio needs to be dynamic. As with effective reporting, one way to avoid escalation of commitment can be to put objective metrics for project success and future funding in place at the time of project launch. For example, the metric might indicate that if a project doesn't achieve $500,000 of benefits in year 2, then the project should be canceled. Furthermore, the real benchmark for continuing a project is not that it hits its own targets, but that it delivers superior returns when compared to other in-flight projects as well as to the strongest business cases that can be made for potential other projects that could be implemented.

Case Study: Efficient Decision Making in Dynamic Markets

A European telecom executive found the pace of change within his industry increased dramatically due to heightened technology innovation and rapidly changing consumer preferences. Reevaluating projects monthly seemed an adequate solution to this, with the overhead of the decision making outweighed by the benefit of a more efficient portfolio. However, in practice, seasoned product managers became experts at pushing their existing projects through and this leads to more projects being continued than was efficient. It created too great a sense of inertia within the portfolio. The solution was to close every project at the end of each month and formally reapprove each project for it to continue, rather than just looking for projects to cut. The impact of this decision was positive in terms of market share and margins. It is interesting to note how an apparently subtle change to a process can have such a broad impact.

THE DANGER OF SLOW DECISION MAKING

Slow decision making, even with a well-defined and robust project portfolio, can dramatically impede performance. Figure 2.2 shows how decision making within an organization can be slow. In addition, organizational inertia can make it much easier to continue projects than to

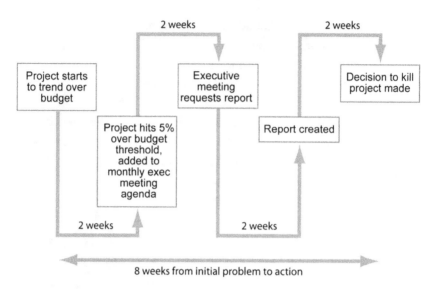

FIGURE 2.2 Danger of Slow Decision Making

kill them. Worse, the larger the project in terms of budget, people, or strategic aspirations, the harder it can be psychologically to say that you were wrong, or at least that forecasts weren't accurate. This problem is particularly acute for external projects. If the CEO has stood on a podium and listed the praises of a key multimillion-dollar project to customers, partners, suppliers, and the media, then reversing course becomes harder. Ironically, these can be the occasions when changing course is most valuable.

This is not to say that big projects are any better or worse than smaller projects. The point is that big projects can be harder to kill than small ones, given the reluctance to accept large-scale failures when there is always the hope that things might turn around next year. When managing your portfolio, pay particular attention to projects that are ongoing, relative to new projects. If anything, you should be more rigorous on existing projects because historical data, rather than mere projections, are available and you should be able to form a better view on whether continual funding is merited. It shouldn't be a foregone conclusion.

No one enjoys failure. However, spotting failure early can be much less expensive than another year of unjustified optimism, especially when you understand the trade-off you are making in funding your low-performing projects at the expense of the others. Better management of your portfolio makes the whole portfolio more efficient. The risk of funding an underperforming project is lower if you know you can identify compelling opportunities elsewhere, rather than just replacing an underperforming project with a similarly underperforming one.

AVOIDING COGNITIVE DISSONANCE

Another psychological trap to be conscious of is that of *cognitive dissonance,* first studied by Leon Festinger (1956) in the context of cults with a belief in UFOs. The research found that the group being studied held a firm belief that the world would end and aliens would save them on a fixed date. Before that date, they were quite a secretive group. After the date passed with no UFO arrival, they became more outspoken about their beliefs, even though there was now demonstrable evidence that those beliefs were false. The theory states that in trying to reconcile the belief in UFOs with no UFO presence, rather than reject the UFO belief, they chose to evangelize their ideas so that others would hold them and provide credibility to their beliefs rather than reject the beliefs outright.

People have obvious difficulties holding inconsistent beliefs. The ability of people to pick up on information that supports their opinions but reject, rationalize, or ignore that which doesn't is widely documented. This occurs unintentionally and is a very common trait if not monitored explicitly. It can cause problems. One obvious application of this phenomenon occurs in the process of monitoring in-flight projects, because the executives who approved those projects want them to succeed. In fact, by approving them, those granting the approval have already expressed that tacit belief, as have the project manager's working hard on those projects. Data on project failure then become inconsistent with that belief, and even a rigorous organization may have trouble recognizing the early warning signs on a key project going off course.

Setting clear, objective, and time-specific targets ahead of time and monitoring progress against them is therefore very valuable. Even more valuable is considering what action will be taken depending on how the metrics pan out. If the criteria for success or failure are not defined ahead of time, then the danger is that the definition of success changes to make sure the project is successful, denying resources that would be better used on another project. This altering of the definition is not the result of malicious behavior but is the way the mind copes with contradictory evidence. Though cognitive dissonance is widespread and hard to avoid, setting clear metrics ahead of time, alongside clear ways of capturing the data, can help reduce the problem. Technology can help here. Reporting criteria can be put in place before the project starts, and workflows can result if the project runs behind schedule or over budget. Creating these processes can enable an organization to avoid excessive optimism about project performance and use objective criteria to identify problems early and clearly.

STRIVING FOR NIMBLE DECISION MAKING

Having a robust strategic alignment process makes portfolio optimization rapid and repeatable. Whereas an ad hoc selection method involves drawn-out discussion without an obvious framework, using a clear process accelerates the selection of projects. This means the portfolio can react to changes as needed. If the budget has to be cut 20 percent, for example, then the same criteria that were used to create the portfolio can be used to cut it while retaining strategic value. If expansion into developing markets becomes a core strategic goal, then the portfolio can be realigned almost instantaneously to support that objective. Once the process is in place, altering the set of projects can be achieved rapidly, leading to fast and effective decision making and a portfolio that changes with the needs of the organization. In this way, the portfolio becomes much more nimble, and there is the opportunity to reconfigure the portfolio rapidly.

KEY QUESTIONS

- Can your organizational strategy be defined in a handful of strategic goals that are applicable to multiple business units?

- Are the strategic goals that you are using likely to remain relevant for the next three years?

- How can you minimize the burden of mapping projects to strategic goals, to make the process of prioritization less onerous?

- Are you using the implementation of a project management system as an opportunity to set aggressive goals across the organization?

SUGGESTED READINGS

R. Charan and G. Colvin, "Why CEOs Fail," *Fortune* (June 21, 1999).

I. Cobbold and G. Lawrie, "Why Do Only One Third of UK Companies Achieve Strategic Success?" *2GC Ltd.* (May 2001).

Leon Festinger, Henry W. Riecken, and Stanley Schachter, *When Prophecy Fails: A Social and Psychological Study of a Modern Group that Predicted the End of the World* (University of Minnesota Press, 1956).

For a rich case study of portfolio decision making at SmithKline Beecham, see Paul Sharpe and Tom Keelin, "How SmithKline Beecham Makes Better Resource-Allocation Decisions," *Harvard Business Review* (March–April 1998).

For further updates on the topics discussed on this chapter, see www.strategicppm.com.

3

The Importance of Planning

Seek first to understand, then to be understood.
Steven R. Covey

KNOWING WHAT YOU ALREADY HAVE

Projects are often inadvertently set up for failure due to insufficient planning. It is often said that failing to plan is planning to fail. Insufficient planning does not mean an absence of planning, but planning that is rushed or is too narrow in scope. This limited planning scope can cause failure or, at the very least, problems in execution. More time invested in the right planning steps can significantly improve portfolio performance.

Before looking to improve your project execution process, it is important to understand the skills that already exist across your organization. An organization that may apparently lack portfolio management expertise will contain numerous project managers practicing different methodologies at different levels of sophistication. The organization will contain strengths in some areas of project management and weaknesses in others. The challenge is to understand the level of project and portfolio management skill within the organization. Knowing which areas to focus on will dramatically improve your performance in creating a system that targets key areas for improvement and avoids overallocating effort to existing areas of strength. As part of this process, simply bringing existing project managers together can help networking and the creation of a project management culture throughout the organization where best practices are developed and shared. This can be done in a variety of ways—for example, through arranging a series of speakers on portfolio management, adding mentoring processes, setting up knowledge management systems for project managers, and organizing social events. In organizations where a formal project management office (PMO) does not exist, projects are, of course, still being managed. Bringing project managers together, regardless of job title, can be extremely valuable to understand the talent and skills that you already have within your organization in addition to identifying important areas for development.

DETERMINING HOW MANY RESOURCES YOU HAVE

In addition to determining the portfolio you want to implement, you need to understand the set of resources you have. This may sound simple—for example, you have $40 million and 200 people over the next 12 months. But it gets complex as the portfolio moves to the detail of implementation (e.g., How much of the $40 million is available in March? How many of the 200 people are not only trained as mechanical engineers but can also manage a customer relationship?). Not all resources are substitutable and all projects are different, so capturing resource skills effectively is key to forecasting which projects can be done and what your gaps and surpluses are. Creating a meaningful taxonomy of the people available within your organization can dramatically improve expertise search and project staffing. This can be done in a lightweight way through unstructured expertise tracking within collaboration tools, or through skills definition within your portfolio management system. In an outsourced environment, there is a little more flexibility around resource management, as it becomes possible to manage the gaps between resource supply and demand through outsourcing. However, the issue then becomes financial rather than resource based.

Case Study: A Portfolio Approval Process

Peter coordinates an IT portfolio for a leading asset management firm. After years of exceptional growth based on a laser focus on meeting customer needs, Peter saw that "processes were not as efficient as they could be." They would typically "drop everything in order to meet tight customer deadlines and, as a result, costs became higher than they could have been." This created a great deal of scope for greater efficiency within IT. The emphasis on meeting customer needs had driven great performance, but some processes were now inefficient as a result.

Peter introduced a stage-gate process for portfolio selection. First, proposals come in—simple ideas typically submitted by product management in the form of a one- or two-page "idea screen." Estimates beyond orders of magnitude are not required at this stage; the goal is to keep the process simple and assess if further research is required. If the idea is thought to have merit, then a small fraction of the total budget is invested in a scoping plan to define how much the total project would cost. This building of the business case is critical to approval of the project and can take a few days to a year, resulting in answering questions and following a process outlined in a 28-page document. The level of detail required increases with the proposal's risk. Riskier proposals require significantly more detailed analysis, given the increased level of uncertainty. This proposal is then reviewed by a cross-functional team, which includes sales, marketing, operations, and IT.

Peter views this business case creation as a critical step in the process. Without it, there's a tendency to be more of a *fixed-price shop* where estimates are fairly consistent regardless of the project in question, which can reduce either the credibility of the estimate or the efficiency of the project. Having a detailed business case process enables a more detailed analysis of the trade-offs between the project costs and benefits to determine the appropriate scope for the project. As Peter emphasizes, the goal

(continued)

is not minimizing cost but ensuring that the maximum benefit is achieved for each dollar of investment.

The projects then go through three stages: design, build, and deploy. At each stage, if the project deviates from its estimate by more than 10 percent, a review is performed. The goal of the review is not necessarily to bring the budget back to its initial estimated value, but to understand how the whole project has changed. Peter mentions examples where changes in scope have increased costs by 10 percent, but also increased the benefits a project can deliver by 25 percent, and he felt that was absolutely the right decision to make. Of course, projects do get killed due to budget overruns, but Peter emphasizes the value of looking at projects holistically and understanding what is driving cost changes, as well as what else is affected when cost changes.

In addition to phased approvals and reviews, monthly reports of project inventory are generated to show what is at each stage of the project process and to enable executives to drill down should they have questions.

The advantage of the process is that ideas are flowing through the system all year long. Budgeting used to be very calendar-oriented, with the result that at certain times of the year, most projects would be in the same phase of planning, causing high demand for certain resources and low demand for others. This volatility made resource management challenging and could slow project development.

Given the greater accountability and impact the process has caused, Peter now wants to extend the process to include the two-thirds of the budget that is spent on operational work. Unlike project work, much of this operational work has to happen, but he wants to better align the level of spending with the perceived benefits. He also plans to extend the concept to outsourcing work. Today, much outsourcing is done on a time and materials basis, but he sees potential to bid out fixed-priced contracts in a more sophisticated way and to monitor the efficiency and benefits realized using portfolio management techniques so that these outsource packages become visible at the portfolio level. The opportunity to bid out the work in a more structured way should also drive cost efficiency. Ultimately, Peter wants to see better alignment between costs and benefits across the organization: "There used to be some assumptions that if something cost $2 million, it was less likely to get funding. But now if we believe in the benefits, we can cut other smaller projects with fewer benefits and find the money."

The other change Peter wants to drive is greater transparency across the portfolio. He says, "We're going to share everything with everybody." There will be different views, but that "doesn't define who can access them." For example, all participants can see the CIO view of IT projects if they want. There will be some exceptions on confidentiality for certain projects, but those will be "very minor." Getting consistent data broadly shared is absolutely critical, since, as Peter says, "Sometimes arguments used to be over the data rather than the decision itself."

(This material is from an interview with the author.)

THE VALUE OF PLANNING

Plans are nothing. Planning is everything.

Dwight D. Eisenhower

Planning is sometimes viewed as dead time when no tangible project process is made, and it is, therefore, not given the time and resources it needs. It is easy, but superficial and ultimately risky, for an executive looking at opportunities to accelerate a project plan to cut the time invested in planning. Any extension of the planning phase is seen as time added to the total project duration—hence, pushing out the completion date of the project. Cutting planning appears to bring the end of the project closer. However, this assumes the project will ultimately succeed, meeting its estimates and the needs of stakeholders, whereas over half of projects fail. Thus, success ought not to be taken for granted, especially where limited planning work has taken place.

Executives can support planning by incorporating sufficient time for it in the overall process. Planning steps can also be built into project approval workflows. It is important to ensure that the time and resources are used productively for planning, rather than diverted to other, apparently more pressing needs. There will often be urgent needs to address in any portfolio. However, this should not mean that longer-term project planning investment is neglected. Cuts to planning phases are often the easiest to implement, but they may carry the highest cost. Greater investment in planning can yield superior results because of more efficient use of resources, important communications and coordination happening earlier, earlier identification of risks, improved integration between tasks, and better definition of overall project scope, to name a few of the most important factors. Also, it is worth considering extending the planning phase for riskier projects where the costs are higher. The net result is likely to be cost savings because possible problems or even project failure can be identified earlier.

This last point is worth stressing. Abraham Lincoln is often quoted as emphasizing the need for disciplined preparation when he said, "Give me six hours to chop down a tree, and I'd spend the first four sharpening my ax." There is no shortage of informed research or well-informed quotes relating to the importance of planning, yet it is so often overlooked. The illusion is that moving quicker toward action will yield quicker overall results, even in very simple tasks. This is seldom the case. It is counterintuitive to imagine that an initial apparent delay might speed project completion, but this is evident from much empirical research. The important thing to note is how widespread project failure is, and thus, the project success should not be taken for granted.

Planning can be supported through detailed business case development before the project starts, ensuring that the project scope is correctly defined, benefits are clearly targeted, and the budget forecast is made with the appropriate level of accuracy. Requiring this documentation can be a prerequisite for project funding or can be made a step in the project approval workflow process. The goal is not to create bureaucracy but to ensure that the right level of planning work is done before project initiation so as to meaningfully improve project success rates.

Alpha Project Managers

In a survey of 5,000 project managers, Andy Crowe of Alpha Project Managers identified the top 2 percent of project managers, calling them *alpha project managers,* and then looked to find what differentiated them from the remaining 98 percent of project managers who participated in the study. It is important to note that 2 percent of 5,000 is 100 and therefore still a fairly small sample, but the results are insightful. Crowe found that this group spent twice as much time on planning than average—21 percent of all project hours. Proper planning makes it possible for a project to accomplish its goals. The statistics are not favorable for new projects. It is important not to jeopardize overall success by shaving a few days off the schedule by cutting the organization planning process. Managers can have a key impact here because often these planning proceeds are determined at the divisional or organizational level and certain planning documents can be made a prerequisite of the project approval process. The point here is not to create a bureaucratic tax on the planning process but to ensure that sufficient time is invested in order to maximize project success.

Collaborative Scheduling

A best practice in the planning process is to build the schedule collaboratively. This is where all members of the team contribute their views on the tasks that need to be done, what order tasks should be done in, and how long particular tasks might take. An approach in which the completion date is the first date on the schedule is a setup for failure. This is the case unless resources are in complete abundance, and even then there are risks. It is highly unlikely that the scope of work required and the team size will match the arbitrarily defined end date. In fact, the chance of this outcome occurring without much friction behind the scenes is virtually zero. However, this is so often how the process commonly starts. By starting with completion dates, the implicit statement is made that timely completion is more important than changes in scope, keeping on budget, and overall quality. For most projects, that simply is not true.

THE TRIPLE CONSTRAINT: TIME, SCOPE, COST

Reading this, you might be wondering if your organization can achieve all of those goals. The answer is maybe. The fact is that project management does require trade-offs. If the completion date is the first thing that appears on the schedule and progress over time is the main thing that is measured, then compromises will have to come in other areas—such as the cost of completion or the scope of work to be done. The classic triple

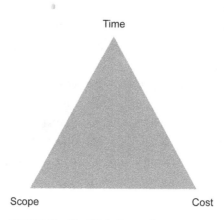

FIGURE 3.1 The Triple Constraint

constraint of project management, shown in Figure 3.1, highlights this trade-off. There are some projects where completion date really is the most important element of the project, but in that case, there must be flexibility in project scope or a substantial budget to ensure on time and successful delivery.

KING CANUTE

This approach might be called the King Canute approach to project management, which is a common flaw. The often cited, but likely historically false, story is that King Canute, a Viking king of England and parts of Scandinavia in the eleventh century, sat on the beach and commanded the tide to turn back. Of course, the tide did not turn back. This act demonstrated to King Canute's flattering courtiers that he was not, in fact, all powerful, and there were some rules even he had to obey. The same is true of management. If your project managers simply tell people when you expect them to complete a task, they may be guilty of the same flaw. Just as kings have to respect tides, so executives cannot always dictate deadlines for complex projects.

The Risk of Setting Deadlines Too Early

In reality, the problem is caused by setting deadlines before the project team is even created. By creating a small project team early to explore the issues and scope of work, the problem of arbitrary deadlines can be avoided, and the team can be kept small enough so that resources are not wasted. However, the real benefit is more predictable project execution because estimates become more reliable and projects finish closer to their intended completion dates. This approach is often referred to as *business case development* and is more or less structured, depending on the organization.

In addition to not making the end date the first date on the schedule, it is worth emphasizing that scheduling should be collaborative. This means working with task owners in constructing the schedule. Simply telling task owners that they must complete a task in four months may or may not be realistic, but by asking them before the schedule is built what they view as a realistic timeline for their tasks, you will arrive at not just a more accurate and attainable schedule but also one that has implicit agreement from those doing the work. A schedule that is broadly agreed to is preferable to one that comes from an isolated, top-down estimation process, regardless of how accurate that process might be. Working with those carrying out the tasks in this way also has the benefit of task owners who are more supportive of the project plan, given their role in creating it. Of course, the main downside is that this collaborative process is more time consuming than a top-down approach to scheduling, but the results are likely to be far better. This is another example of how investing in upfront planning leads to a superior overall outcome for the project.

Student's Syndrome

Student's syndrome, which Eliyahu Goldratt identifies, simply states that people start to work just before a deadline (Goldratt, 1997). Although the behavior is observed widely in students, it is more generally applicable to organizations. The implication is that if you set a deadline, that deadline will be self-fulfilling because work will only start sufficiently ahead of the deadline to get it done with very little leeway to account for last-minute risks and issues. That means that if you set a date for task completion, you may actually risk delaying completion of your project because the project could have been completed earlier. That will never happen once the deadline is in place. In this way, allowing deadlines to be defined by those working on the project, rather than by a top-down edict, may in some cases result in faster completion than if the wrong *top-down date* were allocated, which offered too much buffer in the schedule.

The second is that you may be setting the deadline too early. The task may still get done, but you are forcing trade-offs to make it happen that will show up either in the scope of work completed or perhaps in the quality of the deliverable.

THE IMPORTANCE OF BOTTOM-UP PLANNING

How can these problems be avoided? It is actually fairly simple, but you need to start with a bottom-up planning process. Rather than simply stating when things will be done and backfilling the schedule, put in place a loose structure first and then ask the people doing the tasks to commit to how long it will take them. Just to reiterate the process there: It is important that the individuals doing the work commit to the time they will take, such that the dates in the schedule are dates they have given you, not dates you have told them. That's a key distinction. Clearly, to support this process, we need software that is collaborative so that everyone sees one version of truth from an easily accessible system. Technology can facilitate this. Data do not have to reside on an individual employee's machine but can be located in a central collaborative spot that everyone can access. The key point to note is the democratization of the planning process. Letting others tell you how long they will take before they are committed to the task enables much better estimation in the early phase of project planning.

Buffer

Like the need to devote time to planning, the need to devote space in the schedule to buffer is also contested but can be critical to project success. A buffer is a fixed element in the schedule to separate sections of the project in order to account for delays. Having a buffer enables a schedule to adjust for slippage that is likely to happen, but where the source is not known in advance. Rather than building a schedule that is precisely wrong, the inclusion of buffer permits a schedule that is broadly accurate, and it offers project managers some flexibility in completing work in the context of unpredictable events. The buffer also limits the need to redefine the schedule for every change in a particular task. The buffer can also be used as a metric to measure project progress relative to expectation. A common rule of thumb is to allocate 20 percent of the total duration of the project as a buffer; so a 10-month project would have 2 months of buffer. The project can then be monitored to see how much of that buffer is used over time as a gauge of the likelihood that the project will ultimately deliver on target.

Resource Availability

The first cause of execution failure is inadequate or unavailable resources. One retailer experienced this issue. The problem was not that projects didn't start. They were debated by the relevant committee, and many were approved through a carefully phased approval process. However, some of the more important projects ultimately stalled as the resources they needed were on other projects, with the results that several projects the company thought were in progress were actually floundering without resources needed to make progress. It made the planning process less valuable because whether a project succeeded was determined not by board approval but by its success in negotiating for resources *after* approval had occurred. Two steps are important here:

1. The schedule must be constructed with enough granularity to show the resources that are required.
2. The schedule must include the time the resources are needed.

Schedules can then be combined to view the overall organizational resource requirement. This is one area where technology can have a major impact. Rolling up resources without a centralized repository of plans is time consuming, but technology makes it simple. Of course, there are still risks despite technology. Organizations often have an overoptimistic view of resource availability, or of the handful of unique resources that are truly in demand and that could cause a bottleneck if not planned for in advance.

Operational Work

One common pitfall in fully capturing the availability of your resources accurately is the demands of operational work. Are your engineers working on the projects, taking calls from customers, or advising on in-market products? Typically, there is much ad hoc work that is not part of a project but is critically important and occupies a project resource's time. Of course, this work is important, and if it were cut to enable more projects to get done, the organization would suffer. However, it should be assumed for resource availability that no resource has 100 percent of its time to devote to projects.

Using time-sheeting, organizations can capture an accurate picture of how time is being spent and what proportion of time is spent on *operational* tasks. Without this, an organization's view of resource availability is far too optimistic. Capturing operational work also enables more informed and effective trade-offs to be made; it is known that project capacity is limited by the mass of operational work the organization requires. If more projects are to be undertaken, operational work must necessarily be cut, but more transparency about the nature and scope of operational work must be achieved in order to enable effective decision making. Operational work is often just as valuable as project work. It just seldom receives the same scrutiny that new projects do, and this imbalance can tend toward excessive operational work at the expense of new projects. Making this trade-off more explicit can lead to a more productive organization.

Integration Risk and White Space Risk

Matta and Ashkenas (2003) boil down project failure into two underlying motives: integration risk and white space risk. Integration risk is shown in Figure 3.2. It is the risk that different parts do not come together effectively to deliver a seamless solution to the initial goal or problem. This is often the case because the plan may envision seamless integration, but as the different teams on the project diversify over time in response to local problems and unforeseen issues, so the requirements

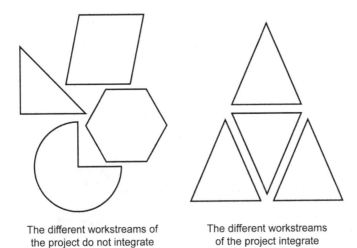

The different workstreams of
the project do not integrate

The different workstreams
of the project integrate

FIGURE 3.2   Integration Risk

may not remain coordinated, and the ultimate deliverable may not hang together.

White space risk, as shown in Figure 3.3, is the risk that something is missing from the initial plan. In many projects, since the scope of work cannot be perfectly known upfront, this risk can be all too real. It is highly unlikely that all the requirements will be known upfront, however. In many cases, the act of carrying out specific tasks may lead to further requirements for the overall project. It is far more likely that work is added to rather than cut from the schedule, and this *white space* can be a significant driver of project overruns.

AVOIDING PROJECT DELAYS

Project delays often happen one day at a time. This is why vigilant monitoring is necessary. Though some delays are the result of new information, such as changes in client requests or realizing a complex technological constraint on a more innovative project, most delays are due to incremental slippage. On a one-year project, if a weeklong task takes just four hours more than expected, which might not be obvious on a daily basis, the cumulative effect would translate into a slippage

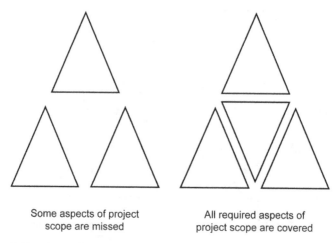

Some aspects of project
scope are missed

All required aspects of
project scope are covered

FIGURE 3.3   White Space Risk

for the overall project of a month, based on eight-hour days. This is why taking time to get estimates correct is so important and why a good understanding of project scope is necessary. If the project scope is wrong, then even the most precise estimates will be off, since you're estimating the wrong thing.

Technology can play a key role. Any project manager collecting progress on a granular basis will have little time to worry about the more strategic elements of the process. Collecting the information in an automated way via electronic status reports or time sheets means that data can be collected with a level of precision that allows a real-time, accurate view to be formed on project progress.

KEY QUESTIONS

- How collaborative is your project management process?
- Is your time-sheeting system capturing project and administrative work?
- Are you using milestones to track your key projects incrementally?
- If you're just looking for a big bang of success at completion, how are you managing risk in the interim?

SUGGESTED READINGS

Naelim Matta and Ronald Ashkenas, "Why Good Project Fail Anyway," *Harvard Business Review* (September 2003).

Andy Crowe, *Alpha Project Managers* (Velociteach, 2006).

For detail on student's syndrome see Eliyahu Goldratt, *Critical Chain* (The North River Press, 1997).

For more on King Canute, see Lord Raglan, "Cnut and the Waves": *Man*, Vol. 60, (January, 1960).

For further updates on the topics discussed in this chapter, see www. strategicppm.com.

CHAPTER 4

Improving Cost Performance

THE BENEFITS OF PORTFOLIO MANAGEMENT

Portfolio management improves cost performance in a number of ways. Portfolio management is relatively uniquely positioned to balance the costs and benefits across some of the most strategically important but relatively high-risk areas of investment. One obvious benefit is the elimination of low-return projects and control of risk at a portfolio level, rather than just on a project-by-project basis. Less obvious, but perhaps more powerful, is the ability to improve cost estimation over time, through rigorous project cost tracking and identification of trends across the portfolio. Projects often run over budget, but a portfolio approach can put in place a process to reduce this problem over time. A portfolio system can also drive greater agility and innovation within the organization, both of which generate financial benefits.

Lagging versus Leading Indicators of Financial Performance

A project portfolio management system is a valuable supplement to a financial accounting system. The system can help align costs and benefits within the organization and often indicates pending financial success or failure before the results are evident through revenues in the financial accounting system. Financial systems are typically a lagging indicator of performance. By definition, any issue picked up by a financial reporting system has already had a financial impact. Conversely, a project portfolio management system creates an opportunity to use a number of leading indicators of financial performance because the probability of a successful outcome can be assessed before financial problems occur.

Portfolio Optimization

The most obvious benefit of portfolio management is that the portfolio can be optimized explicitly. A set of projects can be chosen that offers the best combination of financial and strategic return. If the set of projects were chosen in a more ad hoc manner, adding this discipline would make more efficient use of resources. It would also ensure that resources were available to execute the selected projects. Broadening the set of proposals submitted is likely to increase the breadth of ideas and, ultimately, with more projects to select from, the overall return of the portfolio will increase. Therefore, a robust portfolio management process will translate into superior return on investment across the portfolio.

Taking such a structured approach is important for all work, but operational work is generally lower risk than project work. For operation work, the processes are repeatable and, hence, the cost and outcomes are easier to predict based on prior knowledge and experience. However, project work seldom has this level of certainty. Putting in place a portfolio management system, based on robust estimation and efficient monitoring of results, means that the benefits and costs of some of the most uncertain investments an organization makes can be tracked to ensure greater returns and reduced risk.

In addition to the portfolio balancing benefits through optimization, the process will effectively kill low-return projects that would have slipped through the net had no process existed. Simply eliminating these projects with a rigorous system can be enormously powerful, and it is realistic to expect to achieve this even with a relatively simple portfolio management process.

Greater Agility

Taking a portfolio approach also makes your project process more agile. If the goal changes, projects can be adjusted to meet the new goal quicker than would be possible if a process didn't exist. Without this, projects may be slower to adjust to the goals of the organization, and the adjustment cost is itself an inefficient use of financial resources. Once the set of goals is known and the mapping of the projects to those goals is understood, readjusting the portfolio becomes an easy process. This agility can come in the form of what-if analysis and the ease of comparing multiple portfolios at the time of portfolio decision making. It can also come later in the process, if dramatic changes in market or competitive requirements necessitate a reassessment of the business goals. It is simple to look at what a different set of business goals would mean for the portfolio and understand which projects should be initiated and curtailed to improve the portfolio for maximum strategic impact.

For example, if your projects are locked based on the outcome of an opaque selection process, then once the strategic goals of the organization change (e.g., to cut costs by 10 percent or focus more on European growth), the entire selection process must be redone with the same level of investment and complexity as with the first selection process. However, if projects are already defined in terms of strategic benefit relative to strategic goals, then the process of recasting the portfolio in the light of organizational goal changes is straightforward and a new portfolio can be created almost instantaneously in response to new information. This is not to say that optimizing portfolios and changing strategic goals is something that should be done on a monthly basis. To do so would be likely to create excessive adjustment costs across the organization, and if strategic goals do change frequently, then the goals are more likely to be tactical than truly strategic. Where there is a meaningful shift in the marketplace, the portfolio can react swiftly with the same robust process as in the first selection process. The same agility cannot be offered by ad hoc selection processes. Creating an agile portfolio process is also a great way to drive agility more broadly across the organization.

UNDERSTANDING MARGINAL RETURNS

Simply understanding the marginal returns within your portfolio can help optimize spending effectively. As previously discussed, the goal of any portfolio is to have a strategic impact on the business. The cost of achieving that impact is not constant. Some areas will offer some very attractive returns for low-cost projects (i.e., low-hanging fruit). An example of this might be to take a customer relationship management tool that one sales team is using and broaden usage to other sales teams to achieve the strategic goal of greater customer retention. The tool is already in place, so the cost of rolling it out to other divisions is relatively low, but the impact will be the same as if the tool had been built on a bespoke basis for each division. Some portfolios contain much low-hanging fruit; others will find it much more expensive to realize strategic goals. If the cost of realizing strategic goals is high, that is not necessarily bad. Collecting more ideas through an efficient proposal process might help, but ultimately, there is no reason that achieving strategic goals should have a particular cost. This is why it is important that strategic goals are truly at the strategic level. As long as they don't get to the precise level of tactics, much flexibility is left as to how the goals should be realized, and costs can be optimized a result. If the cost is known across areas of the portfolio, it is enormously valuable in optimizing cost, since resources can be invested in those areas offering superior strategic returns, lowering the cost of the overall portfolio.

In Figure 4.1 the three portfolios all reach the same level of strategic value if all the cost is spent. However, portfolio C delivers most of the strategic value when only a small portion of the cost is invested; after that, the strategic returns diminish. The same trend is true of portfolio

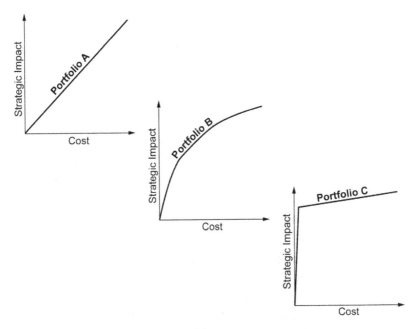

FIGURE 4.1 Marginal Returns across Portfolios

B, but less pronounced, and then the strategic returns to portfolio A are broadly constant for any level of investment. Knowing this, if funds are scarce, some funds might be cut from portfolio C after the point where the rate of return changes and reallocated to A, where the returns do not diminish over time.

The other important aspect is to ensure that a sufficient number of proposals are submitted such that you really do have a choice in the projects you implement. No proposal is good or bad in isolation—it all depends on the number of proposals you have and how they compare against each other. For example, a 12 percent return on investment is attractive if none of your other proposals offers any higher than 5 percent return on investment; but if the other proposals all exceed 20 percent, then 12 percent is less attractive. Therefore, the benefit of the optimization process is partly due to the rigor of the optimization itself, but it is often dependent on a large number of proposals to achieve real results.

ALLOCATING RESOURCES PREDICTABLY

Once the portfolio is defined in advance and projects have business plans with granular data, it becomes possible to see much further ahead for required project resources. This can then enable bulk sourcing of resources that will be needed in large quantities across projects, or on a human capital level, and can enable training and staffing plans to be put in place so that the project needs can be met without costly and resource-intensive expediting procedures. The further ahead you can see, the further ahead you can plan, and the cost of surprises are minimized.

Resource allocation is not just a way to make projects effective through giving them the people they need. It also a key part of developing the human capital within your organization. Doing this right not only helps employee retention and motivation, as employees can be matched with the opportunities they are looking for, but it is also an opportunity to ensure that your organization is developing the skills and experiences it needs to be successful for the long term. Effective resource allocation can drive project success but also help contribute to the success of the organization through the talent of its employees.

For example, if multiple projects needing the same resources at the same time cannot be mitigated by changing project start dates, then that information can be identified sufficiently far ahead to enable a seamless and cost-effective solution to be found. Typically, looking 9 to 12 months ahead is ideal for a mitigation strategy to be found. However, this is dependent on how long resources are committed for their existing work. For example, in a case where a resource is assigned to a project for a number of years, then resource forecasting, too, must take a longer-term perspective.

Solutions might involve hiring more people with a particular skill set or working in a particular geography. It might be to engage in more out-sourcing of a particular area. It might mean training existing employees to take on a particular role or function. There are numerous possibilities to solving these sorts of resource allocation issues, but the key to all of them is starting early. Otherwise, the problem becomes much more challenging in the presence of severe time constraints. The other angle to focus on is that not all resources are geographically substitutable.

A programmer based in Paris may not be willing or able to relocate to a project based in Sydney. Technology and virtually distributed project teams can help here, but still, optimizing resources on a regional basis is the best course of action in the first instance.

Resource forecasting creates a smoother and more predictable approach to resource usage and then makes it easier to better match demand and supply across the organization and lower the cost of product execution.

IMPROVING FINANCIAL FORECASTING

A crucial area for improved portfolio performance comes through improving financial forecasting, specifically in estimating the cost of projects. Effective project management leads to better execution as spend predictions for projects become more accuracy due to robust monitoring. Effective postmortems enable the accuracy of estimates to improve over time. There is no shortage of examples of projects coming in dramatically over budget. The Sydney Opera House cost 15 times its initial cost estimate; the supersonic jet Concorde was 11 times its cost estimate, Denver Airport cost double what was expected, and the Channel Tunnel, between Britain and France, exceeded its costs by 80 percent. Though innovative projects are more likely to come in dramatically over budget, since estimating scope is much harder where new technology is involved, most projects do exceed budget. Furthermore, there is an absence of similar examples of projects coming in substantially less than forecast. Cost overruns are pervasive, and forecasting errors are not random. This suggests that one reason projects are coming in over budget is due to aggressively low initial estimates. Putting in place a robust postmortem process helps mitigate this problem so that there is a process that captures the relative accuracy of forecasts and identifies areas for improvement over time.

Having accurate forecasts avoids costly surprises and makes it easier to finesse the financial outcome of the portfolio. Most important, there will be fewer unwelcome surprises. That is not to say that everything will go to plan; that is unrealistic. But if unexpected outcomes can be reduced by even 5 or 10 percent, then much executive time is saved putting out fires, and those cases that are problematic can receive more focus and attention, leading to swifter and more effective resolution. It also improves budgeting and resource allocation procedures. Resource allocation efficiencies can be particularly helpful. Often, when a project goes behind schedule, the problem is solved through existing resources working more hours, not by adding more resources to the project, which is not good for morale or employee retention, so resource efficiency can yield greater benefits than just cost efficiency.

WINNER'S CURSE

Richard Thaler first identified the concept that if in an auction multiple parties are bidding on the same item, but are all unable to estimate the true value with complete accuracy, then the winner is likely to overpay because the largest overestimate will be selected (Thaler, 1994). The same line of reasoning can be applied to portfolio selection. A number of proposals are bidding to be included in the portfolio, and all costs and benefits are estimated with some magnitude of error. It is likely that projects that are selected are more likely to underestimate cost and overestimate benefits rather than the average. It is therefore crucial that executives scrutinize proposals, use common metrics for assessment, and perform postmortems to capture any systematic biases in estimation.

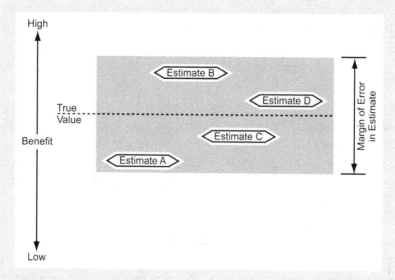

FIGURE 4.2 The Winner's Curse

USING EARNED VALUE

Using earned value can help deliver effective cost estimates. Many projects have accurate data on what proportion of the budget has been spent and how far, chronologically, the project is to completion. However, that is not enough. For example, a six-year project might be six months in, meaning 10 percent of the total time has elapsed and 10 percent of the budget might have been spent, but those data are not sufficient to know if the project is under- or overbudget. To answer that question, it is important to know not how much time has elapsed, but how much work has been done. It is highly unlikely that the volume of work required over the lifetime of the project is uniform. Knowing how much work has been done and how much of the budget has been spent are the data you need to perform an earned value calculation. The relationship between work done and budgetary spending is reasonably constant throughout the life of the project. Knowing this relationship will enable more accurate forecasting across the portfolio.

USING INNOVATIVE IDEAS TO MAKE BETTER USE OF RESOURCES

Whereas many projects require a budget to get results, having a broad proposal process for projects will enable you to capture ideas that may not require financial resources but still offer meaningful strategic impact. These ideas are typically the low-hanging fruit, offering great returns, but it is often hard to identify enough of these valuable proposals. Soliciting a greater number of proposals across the organization will enhance innovation and identify more low-hanging fruit within the organization. It is the megaprojects with large budgets that often require the most analyses and trade-offs to make the right implementation decisions. However, finding more of the simple ideas can be enormously valuable. Allocating resources wisely is imperative, but finding opportunities that require little additional resources for major strategic impact is enormously valuable and can help support an agile, productive organization. It is in capturing numerous, broad ideas from multiple sources that these opportunities will surface. It is not always the case that 10 smaller, innovative projects will outperform a single larger project, but capturing a greater number of ideas enables you to perform that analysis and make the right trade-off based on organizational needs.

ACCESSING SUPERIOR RISK ANALYSIS

Viewing all projects within a portfolio enables superior risk analysis, which can yield tangible financial benefits. For example, for an IT portfolio, any project in isolation may have adequate risk management processes and contingencies in place. However, at the portfolio level, many projects might use the same underlying and risky technology, which then creates aggregate risk at the portfolio level. This is the sort of information that is crucial to capture to enable consistent portfolio delivery. In addition to performing risk management across projects, analyzing risk at the portfolio level is critical to sophisticated and meaningful risk analysis. Given that the risks of various projects will interact with each other at the portfolio level, they may either cancel each other out or magnify the risk. Risk can be captured on multiple dimensions, depending on the characteristics of the organization and their project portfolio, but performing solid risk analysis can make the difference between a few years of good portfolio performance and consistent, long-term portfolio delivery.

For a more advanced analysis of risk, Monte Carlo analysis can be performed on individual projects or the portfolio itself. The name *Monte Carlo* comes from the Monte Carlo Casino, given that the outcomes of a gamble can be modeled in the same fashion. If any project has a particular set of outcomes, such as finishing a month early, on time, or a month late with a probability of each occurring, then Monte Carlo analysis can simulate all the possible outcomes at the portfolio level, showing the likelihood of particular outcomes over all in terms of completion dates, budget, or resource utilization. Monte Carlo modeling requires assumptions about the range of outcomes for a project and their likelihoods, and these data can be hard to determine. However, Monte Carlo analysis does provide a useful tool for analyzing risk across a portfolio.

Duplication of Effort

Creating a portfolio management process avoids doing things twice. This is achieved through a concrete and formal list of the work being done and broad communication of that list throughout the organization. Both of these are necessary to solve the problem; the list of projects will be effective in reducing duplication of effort to the extent it is broadly shared. Avoiding overlapping work creates greater financial efficiency. Of course, the benefit here comes not from creation of the portfolio itself, but from broad communication of portfolio across the organization. Much time is wasted in organizations on duplicative activities, and rolling together similar efforts can magnify their effectiveness. Also, duplication may occur not just between projects but potentially within projects, and here again, greater transparency is valuable. Duplication can also cause confusion within the organization itself, sometimes reducing morale and impeding good-natured collaboration if employees feel a sense of conflict between their group and others within the same organization.

IS DUPLICATION OF EFFORT ALWAYS BAD?

Although duplication of effort is bad from a resource allocation perspective, it is worth considering the opposing view in terms of the benefit to organizational incentives and, hence, improved performance. It can be argued that having the same groups work on similar project can essentially make both groups work harder. This is true in cases where effort cannot be observed, and so it is hard to ensure that people are investing enough effort into the project they are assigned. Here it is argued that the costs of duplication of effort are outweighed by creating superior incentives for those within the organization—though some tasks are performed twice. If they were only performed once, there is a risk that the work would be done much slower or in a less efficient way. This argument is theoretically sound, but some assume major problems with organizational incentives, and that duplication of effort is a necessary solution. The main goal of portfolios should always be elimination of effort, and organizations should look to find better ways to solve incentive problems, which can often be cheaper than performing the same

(continued)

task twice and the morale problems that that can cause. One way of improving performance is through robust portfolio monitoring tools, rather than the creation of internal competition, which produces harmful side effects in terms of morale and can even block transparency as employees become less keen to collaborate with a group they perceive to be competitive, based on their view of the business.

Efficient Monitoring

Enhanced monitoring of projects enables failing projects to be spotted earlier and stopped before further resources are wasted. Monitoring also enables all projects to receive the levels of resources they need in order to succeed. Creating an effective monitoring process minimizes the delay in decision making. Short decision delays can turn out to be a financial problem, as even a few weeks wasted on an underperforming multimillion-dollar project has dramatic financial impact. It is worth noting that this impact is relatively easy to avoid through efficient monitoring. Ensuring that project funding is kept in sync with project performance, project needs, and portfolio management discipline can help achieve this. Exception-based reporting is one measure than can help identify problems early.

Note that efficient monitoring exists not just to kill projects that go irreconcilably off target but also to provide additional resources to projects that can make good use of the resources. Projects, by their very nature, are uncertain. Although some may simply be disappointments, others may reveal larger opportunities than initially supposed, and providing the correct level of incremental resources to those projects can be more impactful than simply weeding out the underperforming projects. Taking this attitude to monitoring is also important in terms of how the process is perceived. Where a monitoring process is viewed as being simply a means of killing failing projects, it will have more of a negative connotation than if it is used to both cut resources in cases of underperformance and add resources where it is warranted based on previously unforeseen opportunities.

Superior Auditing

A project management system can be a valuable source of detail on how money is being spent. Any organization can break spending down into consistent line items, or across groups and division, but a portfolio management system offers rich, additional detail on what the purpose of that spending is and the benefits it is intended to provide. Your accounting system might tell you that your travel and expense budget has grown 7 percent year over year within the engineering organization, but the project management system can help you understand the benefits that spending is supposed to offer and the extent to which those benefits are being realized. While financial accounting systems provide granularity on how your money is being spent, your project portfolio management system can tell you why. Look to your project portfolio management system to provide a way to calibrate spending across initiatives to ensure that investments, particularly in more uncertain areas of the business, are generating the expected results. The project portfolio system is likely to indicate the success or failure of an initiative significantly before the sales or revenue associated with the venture are quantifiable.

Continual Improvement

Implementing an effective system for project portfolio should lead to a step change in financial performance, but more important, it should create a process for continual improvement. The continual cycle of dynamic monitoring of projects, collaboration, and postmortems ensures that the organization can incrementally improve its financial management practices. That continual stream of improvement is likely to exceed the initial step change in financial performance from the implementation of the system itself. However, to realize this benefit, it is necessary to have feedback loops within the system and garner executive support for sufficient flexibility to make incremental changes and refinements to the process over time.

KEY QUESTIONS

- Are you using your portfolio management information to provide leading indicators of business performance?
- How do you ensure the projects you select aren't merely those with the most aggressive estimates?
- What processes are in place to refine the way you manage projects and portfolios?
- How are you optimizing your portfolio in terms of the marginal return for each level of investment?

SUGGESTED READINGS

For an in-depth explanation of the Winner's Curse, see Richard Thaler, *The Winner's Curse* (Princeton University Press, 1994).

For a detailed discussion of risk management across IT portfolios, see F. Warren McFarlan, "A Portfolio Approach to Information Systems," *Harvard Business Review* (September 1981).

For a rigorous analysis of cost overruns in infrastructure projects, see Bent Flyvbjerg, Mette Skamris Holm, and Søren Buhl, "Underestimating Costs in Public Works Projects Error or Lie?" *Journal of the American Planning Association*, Vol. 68 (3), (Summer 2002).

For further updates on the topics discussed on this chapter, see www. strategicppm.com.

CHAPTER 5

Ten Things to Do

This chapter documents the 10 steps for a successful strategic project portfolio management process:

1. Know what you have
2. Build momentum
3. Define business goals
4. Capture ideas
5. Be transparent
6. Prioritize
7. Use efficient decision making
8. Establish communication frameworks
9. Conduct postmortems
10. Improve continually

KNOW WHAT YOU HAVE

Before you start your process, understand the resources and skills that exist across your organization. Project management will occur within businesses without any explicit action from executives. It is core to getting things done. Therefore, assuming you have a blank slate to start with is wrong. Project management, and indeed portfolio management, will occur with the organization, albeit in perhaps an informal, ad hoc, and inconsistent fashion. Understanding how this occurs is critical to building on the organization's strengths and improving on its weaknesses. Even if there are high-profile examples of project failure within your organization, it is likely that there are some best practices within particular groups and divisions that should be retained or even expanded and showcased. Identifying these helps in the process of improving portfolio management processes because it no longer becomes necessary to implement wholesale change with no existing processes to leverage. It then becomes possible to be more tactical in the approach you adopt and create change in phases focusing on the areas of greatest return on investment.

In addition to helping you decide where to focus, performing an effective portfolio management skills audit will demonstrate the benefits and opportunities from implementing a portfolio management process, as well as highlight how it will align with the organization's existing processes. Therefore, understanding what you have can make improvements to the portfolio management process more targeted and impactful, while at the same time helping demonstrate the key areas of need for portfolio management improvement to your stakeholders. Indeed, a successful audit can also help identify potential stakeholders and advocates for change. This initial capabilities audit can also serve as a benchmark to assess improvements in the portfolio process over time. For all these reasons, understanding your existing competencies and processes across groups and divisions is a valuable initial step in a portfolio management process.

BUILD MOMENTUM

There is much discussion of carrots and sticks as motivational techniques, but carrots generally work better in well-functioning organizations, particularly within a distributed process such as portfolio management. The more you can do to demonstrate that portfolio management is an exciting and powerful process—not just for executives, but for all stakeholders across the organization—the more effective the system will be. The enemy of any project portfolio management system is stale data, which destroy credibility and make the process counterproductive. The way to avoid misleading data is to ensure buy-in across the organization. Momentum can be built in different ways, but demonstration of early successes and then broader roll-out is an effective strategy, rather than trying to attempt too much at once. This momentum also lessens the burden on the initial team championing the portfolio process. As groups adopt the process, the initial team should become advocates for it and provide demonstrable evidence of success.

Providing benefit for all levels of the organization supports momentum. The more of the organization that feels real benefit of the system, the more the system will be supported. Transparency helps here: The more people can see the data, the more they will be able to benefit from it. Ensure that the portfolio management process doesn't just result in an executive dashboard. The process must help create a culture where different and previously separated teams can share and collaborate on project information. This will enable different teams to benefit from the system in various unforeseen ways and multiply the system's effectiveness. Figure 5.1 depicts a process for building momentum through a deployment.

DEFINE BUSINESS GOALS

Everything stems from the creation of business goals. Without it, project prioritization is arbitrary and potentially misdirected. Defining appropriate business goals is the critical first step—otherwise, prioritization lacks structure. It also creates the risk that project stakeholders' ability to influence will become more important than the proposal itself, and such a process is unlikely to be one that inspires others to get involved and support it. Defining these goals at a high level is crucial. If the goals are simply tactics, then there is less flexibility in the portfolio and it becomes harder to find creative solutions to achieve the goals of the

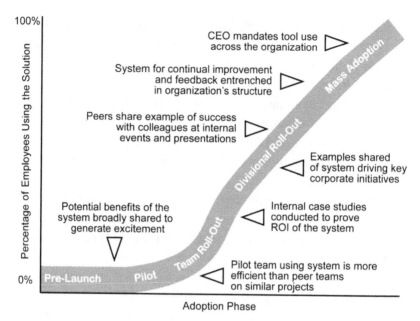

FIGURE 5.1 Building Momentum

business. Without clear and broadly shared and supported business goals, it becomes impossible to create a portfolio that will have the required strategic impact.

CAPTURE IDEAS

The more ideas you capture, the stronger your portfolio will become. Increased choices improve your options for finding opportunity and managing risk across the portfolio. A variety of ideas is important, and proposals should be captured broadly from across the organization. If all ideas come from the same source, be it a particular division, role, or geographic area, then the creativity across that set of ideas is likely to be lower. Creative ideas not only offer cost efficiencies but can also be a source of differentiation for the business to win against the competition. For example, Netflix has grown dramatically by using the creative business model of shipping movies through the mail, based on an online movie queue set up by customers. The model also changes the pricing structure for movies, as customers pay a subscription fee for the number of movies they have shipped to them at any one time. Netflix is now also using an online distribution model, in addition to the mail service. This continual innovation has enabled Netflix to continue to acquire customers from entrenched competitors.

BE TRANSPARENT

Transparency has many benefits. A transparent process is more visible and therefore likely to be improved, because the set of people who can observe the process and refine it is larger. A transparent process is likely to enjoy greater support and buy-in. Opaque processes and black boxes are seldom magnets for ideas and voluntary engagement and cooperation. In addition, the cost of creating information is generally fixed, but the benefit multiplies as the number of people it is shared with increases. In this way, transparency can help magnify the benefit of the insight that the portfolio system creates. Transparency can also overcome common portfolio pitfalls such as duplication of effort driven by lack of awareness.

PRIORITIZE

It is important that the prioritization process is both robust and clear. A transparent process of prioritization is necessary to get buy-in for the process and avoid duplication of effort. If everyone is aware of which projects are happening, then it is less likely that two projects are inadvertently doing the same thing. Making the process clear and accessible also makes it easier for participants to suggest improvement and understand how the system works so that proposals are higher quality and there is a greater degree of understanding of the overall goals of the process. A clear process is also likely to be less time consuming. Disputes will be less about the process itself, which may not be productive, and more about achieving the desired outcome for the business, which can be extremely desirable. By having a clear process, you can align even activities that are not explicitly part of the process with the process goals.

The prioritization must be linked to the strategic goals of the business and must ensure that projects are selected as a set, not as the best set of projects in isolation. Considering projects as a set will create a more efficient portfolio from a risk management and cost management standpoint.

USE EFFICIENT DECISION MAKING

Reporting is critical to an effective portfolio management system. Whereas collecting up-to-date and accurate data is a challenge, building an effective reporting system is relatively easy. Reports should answer specific questions and be tied to specific processes. Reports that simply look appealing or provide a host of data without underlying meaning are ineffective. Therefore, reports should be the outcome of your portfolio management processes.

It is important to consider the following key report types:

- *Single-page project report.* Using a consistent format for project status reports is important. Doing so means less time can be spent on the layout and more attention can be paid to the data within the report. Each project summary should be contained on a single page or screen, with top-level details and the contact information for the project manager and project owner provided should questions arise. The data should also be time-stamped.

- *Budgetary information.* This provides aggregate roll-up on budgetary status across projects with the ability to drill-down into individual projects.

- *Project dashboard.* One-line summaries of the projects currently in execution, filterable by important grouping such as division or project sponsor. Often these lists can run to thousands of projects, so by default, filter on the poorly performing projects (such as behind schedule on the status indicator) first, as it is likely those projects are of most interest and require most attention.

- *Resource allocation view.* This is a view of current resource availability and utilization for the coming 12 months.

- *Strategic alignment.* This provides a view of the strategic goals of the business and how the current projects contribute to them.

- *Flexible pivot table capabilities.* No project report or set of reports will capture everything that is needed, even where drill-down capabilities are available. Using a drag-and-drop pivot table–style analysis on the inventory of projects or proposals can help executives and others find the information that they need to answer a particular question and also lead to creative analysis to produce new report types to further support decision making.

Case Study: Driving a Product Launch

Denis, a marketing manager, drives a project to coordinate a brand launch for a large online business, so he engages with a vendor to build an Enterprise Project Management solution, then builds a business case for other groups throughout the organization to build their own plans, with interdependencies, on the new portal. Approximately 130 people are involved in the launch, which culminates in a single-day event as the new brand goes live. Therefore, coordination across different teams and groups is very important, since some activities can only happen after other work is complete and delays to some activities can have knock-on effects for the whole schedule.

Creating a consolidated project dashboard that everyone can see provides a clear source of project updates, as well as the ability to build summary reports to update executives on the high-level status of different workstreams. In addition to the schedule, a decision list is presented, which highlights key decisions that have been made or are pending, so that they are visible to all team members. The dashboard also makes good use of soft metrics. Most dashboards have the RAG indicators—red for late, amber for slipping, and green for on target. However, Denis's dashboard adds soft metrics to complement this—for example, a task may be late, but the project manager knows that the issue is already fixed and there will not be any repercussions for the main schedule. Another column of indicators

(continued)

captures the *project manager perception*—a custom column that highlights how confident the project manager is that the task (often from needing input from another team) will be finished on the baseline date.

The combination of a dashboard with hard and soft indicators and the list of key decisions beneath provides a one-stop solution for all interested parties in the brand launch. The dashboard also provides a framework for the weekly brand launch meeting, and even though the dashboard provides the high-level summary, the various project subplans are all in the system, so it is easy to drill down and just focus on the tasks that are due in the next week out of the hundreds of tasks that are contained within the system.

ESTABLISH COMMUNICATION FRAMEWORKS

Although communication itself is challenging to mandate and control, providing effective tools for communication can dramatically improve project performance. This is because communication is the critical ingredient to project success. An easy-to-use set of communication and collaboration tools is critical, spanning the latest e-mail technologies to portals that end users can customize, along with tools such as wikis and instant messaging that support teams communicating in the way that is most appropriate to their specific situation. The most obvious benefit is that more communication is better than less, things are less likely to be poorly communicated, duplication of effort is avoided, and alignment can process efficiencies. It addition, quicker communication can speed project progress. If a key decision maker needed to make a decision related to the critical path cannot be found for a day, the whole project will be delayed by day. Speeding communication can accelerate the entire project.

CONDUCT POSTMORTEMS

The interesting trait about project management is not that projects go overbudget, but that this problem is consistently repeatedly. Project portfolio processes should be made more efficient over time, and it is postmortems that can uncover these opportunities. Without postmortems there is no mechanism for improvement. Postmortems are also critical for ensuring that estimates are reliable. If there is no feedback loop, then there is little incentive for estimates to be as accurate as they can be, since no process is making sure that they are. If there is a tendency toward overestimation in some areas and underestimation in others, a series of postmortems can identify these biases. Once there is awareness of these biases, correcting them is relatively easy.

Case Study: A Postmortem Process

Lisa, a PMO director at a North American consumer goods company, applies the following postmortem process. Upon project completion, a lessons-learned survey is sent to participants involved in project. This focuses on the core project team, sometimes including members of the extended team and the project steering committee, as appropriate. The survey asks about each phase of the project, such as requirements gathering, the technical construct, the testing phase, and the ultimate definition of success. The survey is intentionally not people-focused to enable the team to hone in on process improvement. The comprehensive nature of the postmortem document offers a mechanism for a formal audit of the end-to-end process, and enables the group to discuss as a team what worked and what didn't. The focus of this postmortem process is to drive process improvement. The results of the survey and discussion are consolidated into a lessons-learned document. These lessons-learned documents are open for all to see. They are written in a way that is very process-focused. For example, it might help people learn how to set up projects well at the beginning of a project. At the end of the year, lessons learned are consolidated into a master document.

IMPROVE CONTINUALLY

Postmortems must be used as a catalyst for improvement. Portfolio management is an organic system. Each component impacts the others, and change should be constant to ensure that the portfolio is reacting to business needs and changes in organizational conditions.

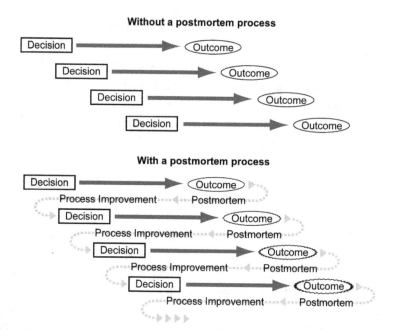

FIGURE 5.2 Feedback between Decisions and Outcomes

Any static process will be overtaken by an inferior process with the capacity to improve over time, as long as that improvement is consistent over time and the processes are in place for many years. Project portfolio management is a relatively new field. Willingness to embrace new ideas and thinking is key to realizing the best results. Since there is no single best way to manage a particular portfolio, because it depends on the needs and goals of the organization, adaptability is critical for long-term success. Figure 5.2 illustrates the importance of postmortems in creating an impact feedback process.

Postmortems are key to improvement, but so is a culture of pragmatic opportunism and a willingness to experiment. Improvements need not wait until after the project has ended, and all those involved in the project should be empowered to make the changes needed to drive improvement. Moderate tolerance for risk is also desirable, so that changes can be introduced and tested with particular groups or divisions and then implemented more broadly if they succeed, or reversed if they fail.

Taking this level of risk with process change is desirable, relative to the risk of maintaining a static process—which will almost inevitably decline in usefulness over time if no action is taken.

KEY QUESTIONS

- Do you know the relative strengths of your organization in terms of portfolio management skills?
- How are you driving excitement and momentum around your portfolio management process?
- How are your portfolio reports linked to actionable decisions and outcomes?
- Is your process sufficiently transparent?
- What is your postmortem process?

CHAPTER 6

Best Practices

KEYS TO PORTFOLIO SUCCESS: WHAT ARE YOU MONITORING?

Anything that can be measured can be improved. However, organizations don't always do sufficient monitoring. Research by Marakon Associates in 2005 showed only 15 percent of organizations actually track performance against benchmarks. Worse, strategic multiyear initiatives are the least likely to be tracked in a quantitative, objective manner. For smaller organizations, the absence of such a heavy process might be understandable, but the introduction of even a lightweight process within a large organization can have tremendous value, relative to no process at all. The main reason for this is that a portfolio of projects contains tens or even hundreds of projects with broadly similar characteristics: goals, allocated resources, budgets, and so on. Monitoring these in an ad hoc manner is likely to be inefficient at best, and leaves important issues to slip through the cracks at worse. A monitoring system is needed. Lack of measurement also harms the goal creation process because there are then no feedback loops. Without a feedback loop, the opportunity for improvement diminishes and the credibility of the process itself may also be put at risk because feedback that the process is providing the value it claims is necessary for the process to continue. Implementing a process helps avoid this problem, but the process need not be particularly onerous. Exception-based processes can help here. It may not be necessary to go into detail on all projects, but ensure that those projects in the portfolio that are materially behind schedule are followed up on and that everything that is planned is tracked.

A process that includes all projects but only invests significant time in those projects that are off target is exception-based reporting. Exception-based reporting means that only projects that pass a certain threshold are reviewed—for example, projects that are more that 10 percent behind schedule are highlighted and require a decision as to whether corrective action is needed. This saves time in not having to review all projects in a detailed manner, as the projects that are on track are not analyzed to the same level of detail. It also means that attention can be drawn to projects when problems occur, not necessarily when the review meeting happens. Having alerts set up should a project go off target means that stakeholders can be notified in real time, rather than having to check the dashboard or waiting to receive the data within a particular review meeting. This can improve the speed of response, which can help drive more agility in portfolio management. It also creates a feedback loop, which can help drive improvement. Driving the process by alerts rather than by scheduled meetings can be helpful, even if the review meeting is monthly, if a project starts to go off target the day after the review meeting. By the time of the next review meeting, it might be a month behind schedule, which for a six-month project likely means the project has severe issues. Alerts also work well for the late stages of projects—as delivery is close, more monitoring attention is often needed, and alerts can be configured to support that, without requiring the need to scrutinize all projects in detail as they approach delivery. An efficient system of alerts ensures that management focuses on the right issues systematically, rather than spreading themselves too thinly across the whole portfolio. Figure 6.1 highlights the key areas needed for success.

Area	Definition	Next Step
Demand management	Capturing an extensive list of project ideas from different sources	Utilizing accessible, Web-based forms to capture project proposals
Strategic alignment	Mapping projects to predetermined strategic goals to determine which projects to implement	Optimizing projects based on strategic alignment
Transparency	Avoiding duplication of effort and enhancing communication by making project metrics public within the organization	Creating online real-time project dashboards and scorecards
Communications	Providing tools to allow employees to communicate using different media	Exploring instant messaging, presence indicators, Web-based meetings, and collaboration portals
Monitoring processes	Providing clear criteria for exception-based reporting and effective project postmortems	Structuring workflow to underpin reporting processes and using collaboration portal to support postmortems

FIGURE 6.1   Keys to Portfolio Success

BUILDING LEGITIMACY THROUGH EFFECTIVE MONITORING

Not tracking project results creates a vicious circle: If results are not tracked, then how can the strategic planning process have credibility? It is likely that it doesn't, and over time, the risk is that estimates are used more as a means of making a project appear worthy of funding than as a mechanism for robust estimation of future results. Without tracking, there is no mechanism to make sure initial estimates are realistic. This is crucial because there can be a tendency to provide estimates that are artificially low in order to gain project approval, especially where there is no monitoring process in place to capture this. What's to stop the *winner's curse* of the most inflated projections getting funded based on elaborate but dubious projections, rather than the best project with credible and realizable, if more modest, strategic benefit? If you are not monitoring performance, then not only will execution performance inevitably deteriorate but your selection process will lose legitimacy and will ultimately become a time-consuming charade. An ornate portfolio selection process is no real value without proper tracking of execution. In fact, it is potentially worse than no process at all. Execution tracking enables you to realize the full benefits of your portfolio selection process. This process also enables your process to adapt and improve over time. Without a feedback mechanism through benefits capturing, supplemented by a strong postmortem process, this is unlikely to occur.

Monitoring also creates the critical link between words and actions. Many organizations have strategic goals, yet few track them in a quantifiable way. Given that CEO failure is often due to execution and not strategy, this sort of tracking is imperative. Lack of tracking not only risks jeopardizing the selection process; it may also put at risk the whole strategy of the business. Measuring progress in a systemic fashion is key.

CAPTURING WHAT YOU NEED

Monitoring needs to be balanced. Not monitoring project success can cause sloppy execution, which is costly. However, monitoring too much can cause a project to drown under the weight of its own status updates. Collect data frequently, but only at the level required to make a decision. Budgeting is one example. It is important to define what constitutes a meaningful budget overrun and measure to that level. If you only care about the aggregate budget, then breaking out the full budget by line item on a monthly basis is overkill and can distract from the decision and monitoring process that you're trying to follow. Where data collection is not automated, track only what you intend to act on; more detail can always be captured subsequently should an issue arise.

However, effective automation and drill-down reports can be a real time-saver here and can eliminate the trade-off entirely because tracking happens automatically as a result of other actions. If your time sheet system can feed project management data into the system, then no incremental effort is needed to build reports and your reporting system can effectively pivot the data on a real-time basis. For whichever reports you chose to collect, the burden of capturing data across the organization remains fixed and relatively light. Reporting is one area where the benefits to a portfolio management process are obvious, rather than rolling up numerous ad hoc spreadsheets, and an effective and broad system for data capture can save time and increase visibility into business performance. Without it, you must be very precise in the data you collect in order to avoid overburdening the organization or hitting material data-quality issues.

However, don't let a broad reporting system allow you to neglect the process of effective reporting. A mass of data is not the same as a report. Even if executives can drill down into real-time portfolio information, that is too ad hoc to be a process for keeping projects on track, and you will still need a structure of reports at consistent intervals to ensure that projects remain on target and to identify trends throughout the portfolio that may not be meaningful for an individual project, but are causing problems at the portfolio level. Of course, having a self-service aspect to data visualization is critical to success, as the data can answer more questions than any set of reports could provide. More important is having your core reports defined to drive projects forward.

The other aspect of a report system is the link between reporting and methodology. Ideally, key reporting metrics should be broadly applicable and not encourage the use of a specific methodology. However, if you are using one consistent methodology, then your reporting system offers one way to enforce it. There is no right answer here, and methodologies are generally driven by organizational preference. However, the metrics you track can have a significant influence on the methodology your organization uses to track projects.

CREATING AN EFFECTIVE DASHBOARD

Once you know what you are looking to measure, it helps to create a one-screen dashboard that captures the relevant information. The term *dashboard* uses an automotive analogy to convey the ideas of getting all relevant information simply summarized in one place. This gives an opportunity to effectively summarize project data in an attractive and transparent fashion. Usage of color and graphical indicators can highlight areas of importance, and the best dashboards combine current and trended information to identify patterns. Dashboards can be done as printouts, but having the data presented online ensures that they are up to date because updates are real time and the data in the system are always current. Online dashboards can also be created to enable drilling down so that the summary data are presented but if more information is needed, the executive can double-click on a project to see full detail on risks, issues, budget, the project manager, team, and current tasks. This type of drill-down setup helps ensure that the initial dashboard is concise but the information is all easily accessible when needed.

Not all dashboard metrics need to be quantitative. Team morale is often hard to define and cannot easily be pulled from a reporting system like the most recent cost data, but it is important and can be very useful in monitoring how the portfolio is progressing. Ensuring that the right data are captured on a dashboard is critical, regardless of whether that data can be pulled out of a database. Also, with broad survey technology, it does become easier to leverage the *wisdom of crowds* across the project team. No one individual or data point may be the single source of truth on the morale of project team, but by anonymously surveying the project team and aggregating the results, team morale can be tracked on an ongoing basis. Technology makes the collecting of this sort of data increasingly simple.

SHARING INFORMATION

Often, organizations are very sensitive to the information shared with junior employees. However, there are few examples of company failure due to information leakage, and there are numerous cases of failure where the broader organization simply did not know what senior management was doing. Many organizations fail because of misguided decisions based on out-of-date assumptions, where more junior employees might have influenced management if they had visibility into the process. Opening up access to decision making can help improve the outcome of decisions. One of Sam Walton's innovations at Wal-Mart was to share detailed innovation with his store-level employees to improve decision making and create a greater sense of empowerment across his organization.

Often, the reason information is not shared is because access to information is a source of power, and limiting access to that information can enhance an employee's status. However, this line of reasoning, to the extent it is true for the individual, based on a very narrow definition of success, is unambiguously negative for the organization. Furthermore, the same information-hoarding behavior that individuals can display can be just as harmful at the group or divisional level. All forms of these information fiefdoms should be prevented. The other line of reasoning is that legal risk means that information cannot be shared. This is valid for some types of information ahead of earnings announcements, brand launches, or patent filings, but this only applies to a limited set of data and does not prevent sharing of strategic goals, organizational process, and product-level information with a broad set of employees. Indeed, in many cases, sharing this information gives it legitimacy. How can an organization have a true strategic goal if only a subset of the employees know about it? One of the advantages of a clear portfolio management process is that, as managers have broader access to a broad and accessible set of data, employees, too, can be giving access to the same information, which provides a greater sense of motivation and understanding of the business goals.

SETTING REVIEW MEETINGS

Capturing data, such as in a dashboard, often needs a process to make it successful. A monthly portfolio review meeting helps make the collection of data actionable. The meeting can review the dashboard, and particularly any significant changes related to the dashboard, and help address them. Knowing that the dashboard will be used in this way makes the dashboard meaningful. Simply creating a well-designed dashboard in the hope that someone will find and act on it is wishful thinking if there is no process to support it. Ahead of creating the dashboard, consider decision thresholds and the resulting actions. If an indicator turns red for a particular project, what would be the result? If no action would be taken, then why is that piece of information on the dashboard? If the resulting decision is ambiguous, then clarifying the course of action ahead of time can be enormously helpful, given that making decisions in the moment can become a lot more heated. It is also important to consider what other information could result in portfolio actions being taken. If the information is material, consider adding it to the dashboard, even if the data in question are not quantitative. For example, the project management might have a *perception* of project performance. Ideally, the dashboard should capture all aspects of project status. If a project could be killed despite having a completely positive dashboard performance, then either the dashboard or the organization is not working effectively.

If a monthly meeting feels too time consuming, the review can be electronic—sending out the dashboard in an e-mail to draw attention to it can be just as effective for driving awareness, though e-mail is a less effective tool should issues arise. Even in cases where the meeting is in person, submitting content electronically ahead of the meeting can lead to a more productive discussion in the meeting if people are familiar with the content in advance. Using alerts can help automate this distribution process ahead of your meeting.

THE TRANSPARENT ORGANIZATION

Often, organizations lock down the permissions or access rights that are given to their employees too finely. Security is based on minimizing the negative consequences of information leakage, rather than maximizing the positive benefits of information sharing within the organization among employees. Of course, with improvements in intranet search and in tagging and taxonomy systems, content will be more discoverable and permissions policies therefore become more important. Simply thinking something is secure just because it is hard to retrieve will not succeed in the future to the extent it ever succeeded in the past.

Nonetheless, consider making various project key performance indicators (KPIs) public to a broad set of employees within the organization. This will help foster new ideas for projects and improve project collaboration. Ideally, disclosure at the KPI level should not reveal confidential information and more granular permissions can be set on drill-down financials. Generally, providing more information on project performance and processes can help with the goal of avoiding duplication of effort, and provide a further opportunity to emphasize the goals of the organization. Of course, as with any security discussion, it is important to remember that this applies just to the rights of employees within the organization, giving public access outside the organization to project plans and progress is likely to pose another set of risk/reward trade-offs and is not part of this discussion, as the security threats posed by nonemployees can be much more severe.

FROM MONITORING TO ACTION

Even the most well-designed dashboard is only data. Projects require decisions to reach effective outcomes and maintain effective performance. Often when dashboard indicators move in the wrong direction, the appropriate action can be ambiguous and confusing. Optimism, or even delay, can lead to important actions not being taken soon enough. In some cases, a late decision can be worse than a faster decision based on less precise information. One useful exercise can be to define decision rules based on the dashboard at the time the dashboard is created. The benefit of doing this is that otherwise coming up with decisions as the data come in results in very complex discussions. For example, it could be decided that any project with a budget overrun of 50 percent will be stopped, or that any project more than six weeks behind schedule must receive executive approval to continue. These rules are only examples, but tying decisions to the dashboard directly makes the dashboard more purposeful and leads to effective outcomes. The challenge is to define an effective governance system based on the dashboard metrics. Of course, the system need not be absolute, but there is more clarity when decisions about how projects should be treated are made in advance of major slippages and cost overruns, rather than after the fact.

UNDERSTANDING ORGANIZATIONAL COMPETENCIES

The best organizations not only understand where they want to go with portfolio management, but also have a clear understanding of their competences today across different divisions. For example, it is good to understand that your organization lacks a process for portfolio management, but it is preferable to break the issue down into its core components to understand the steps required to get there. For example, is the immaturity of the organization's portfolio management driven by lack of defined strategic goals or an ill-defined proposal submission process? In practice, it is likely to be a combination of factors, and the factors are not binary but, rather, measured in degrees. Truly understanding the skills across different divisions within your organization is powerful. You can identify the major areas for improvement, share best practices, and create a clear road map to achieve your goals through incremental, manageable steps, rather than setting a broad direction but failing to understand the steps to realizing that vision. Some of the key competencies to access are outlined in Figure 6.2.

MAXIMIZING INTEGRATION, MINIMIZING TRAINING

Training is necessary to make any system or process work. Without training, people simply will not know what to do. However, the costs of training can be minimized by making the tool as intuitive as possible and leveraging systems your employees already know and are comfortable with. There is often opposition to having to learn something completely new, but if the portfolio management process works within existing tools, it is likely to be more broadly supported and used. One example is personal task tracking. An employee who works on projects may track personal tasks through the task list in their e-mail tool, such as Microsoft Outlook. If their project task information can appear within the same system, then it becomes much easier for employees to update their project status, leading to richer data within the system. Task updates are not the only example, but the more the portfolio system can integrate with commonly used tools within your organization, the greater the likelihood of real success in terms of broad usage of the system. Of course, offering this level of integration is not a complete substitute for

Competency	Definition
Strategic goal definition	Clearly defined, agreed on, and shared goals to drive organizational decision making to map projects to measure both strategic alignment and strategic contribution
Proposal submission	A means of capturing business ideas broadly across the organization in a consistent and standardized manner
Business case development	Formalized steps to add sufficient detail to proposals to enable portfolio selection decisions to be made (this includes mapping projects to strategic goals)
Resource forecasting	Ability to forecast supply of the resources required for projects through the planning horizon (typically 12 months or more) with reasonable accuracy
Resource assignment	The ability to supply people with the right skills for a selected project
Estimation	Ability to forecast the resources required for projects credibly, consistently, and with increasing accuracy over time
Transparency	Sharing the portfolio process with the broader organization to promote engagement and understanding
Executive buy-in	An understanding by senior decision makers within the organization that the portfolio process is desirable, such that it enjoys broad support and it underpins executive decision making
Governance	A step-by-step approach, or workflow, to chart the progression of a proposal through the submission process consistently
Risk assessment	A process to determine and mitigate risks across the portfolio that are distinct from the risks that occur at the individual project level
Refinement	The ability and desire to refine and simplify the process over time
Agility	Ability to react to material changes in business circumstances where the portfolio is impacted
Execution	The ability to execute on the selected projects and realize the forecasted benefits (the area of execution contains many critical subcategories, which are not discussed here)

FIGURE 6.2   Example Competencies for Strategic Portfolio Management

training. It will still be necessary in many areas and is often critical for overall success, but where familiar tools can be used in the context of project portfolio management, it minimizes complexity for the users of tools within your organization.

EMPLOYING BEST PRACTICES BY ORGANIZATIONAL TYPE

Many best practices remain true regardless of the organization in question. Some corporate cultures may struggle with creating sufficient transparency if their organization is more hierarchical; others may not be able to streamline decisions as effectively as they would like based on pervasive frameworks for decision making. It is also important to define whether your organization is more project oriented, knowledge management focused, or service oriented. This taxonomy can help you think about how best practices apply to your organization. Examples in Figure 6.3 show how best practices might be adapted to certain types of organizations. It is easier to state what to emphasize and more controversial to state what is less important. The key is to understand that areas of focus must adapt to the type of business in question.

Organization Type	Example Industry	Example Business Group	Areas to Emphasize	Areas of Less Importance
Project driven	Mining	Operations	Strategic alignment	Organizational transparency
Knowledge management focused	Pharmaceuticals	R&D	Broad information sharing	Monitoring processes
Service oriented	Management consulting	Sales	Communications	Strategic alignment

FIGURE 6.3   Sample Business Scenarios

KEY QUESTIONS

- How does your organization think about the risk of information not being shared and the corresponding risk of duplication of effort when information is not shared?

- How can you simplify your project dashboard? What information do you collect that you don't use?

- Which metrics are you monitoring and taking action on?

- How is your portfolio management process adapted to your organizational type?

- Does your portfolio management process have the appropriate level of transparency?

SUGGESTED READINGS

For a thorough review of recent academic literature on the factors determining project success, see R. Müller, M. Martinsuo, and T. Blomquist "Project Portfolio Control and Portfolio Management Performance in Different Contexts," *Project Management Journal*, Vol. 39 (3): 28–42.

For a detailed discussion of the winner's curse, see Richard Thaler, "The Winner's Curse," *Journal of Economic Perspectives*, Vol. 2 (1) (1988).

For more on the transparent organization and other broad technology trends, see Daniel Rasmus and Rob Salkowitz, *Listening to the Future*, John Wiley & Sons, 2008.

For further updates on the topics discussed on this chapter, see www.strategicppm.com.

CHAPTER 7

Ten Things to Avoid

This chapter documents the 10 things to avoid for a successful strategic project portfolio management process:

1. Moving too fast
2. Allowing heavy processes
3. Relying on the big bang
4. Not tying reports to actions
5. Not killing projects
6. Failing to calibrate estimates
7. Missing scope changes
8. Compartmentalizing information
9. Providing inadequate resources
10. Planning insufficiently

MOVING TOO FAST

Achieving a full project portfolio management system is a challenge. It can be frustrating to move slower than maximum speed in terms of rolling out tools and processes throughout the organization. However, taking a more measured approach can help adoption, as it becomes easier for the organization to digest the required changes. It is tempting to believe that moving at a breakneck speed will result in a faster implementation. Although a sense of urgency is certainly helpful, it is important to assess and respect the bandwidth of the organization to understand change. This is particularly important for areas where broad adoption across a large group of people is required. The time for the organization to understand all the required changes can be slow—here, focusing on tools that the organization is familiar with and are easy to use can accelerate this process. A phased approach can make the required process manageable—each phase should be relatively simple and produce demonstrable results. Introduction in this manner is likely to be more successful.

ALLOWING HEAVY PROCESSES

An onerous process can create a system where a portfolio management consumes more time than the benefit it provides. This can be particularly important in the initial stages when the benefits of the portfolio management process are less apparent, and resistance to change from familiar practices is being felt most acutely. This leads to a situation where only the most committed participants are providing data into the system, and lack of a comprehensive range of data then prevents retrieval of meaningful data from the system. The key to a successful system is to make data capture easy—and if possible, automated as Figure 7.1 shows. Without data, the system is meaningless. It is important to only capture data you will need, not data that might be useful at some undefined point at the future. This is particularly true where data collection requires effort. Where this is the case, the data should be scrutinized to ensure that they are valuable. It is also helpful to consider the process

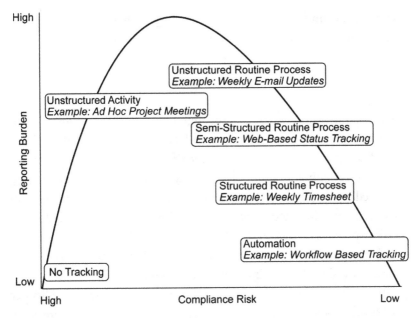

High

Reporting Burden → Low

Unstructured Routine Process
Example: Weekly E-mail Updates

Unstructured Activity
Example: Ad Hoc Project Meetings

Semi-Structured Routine Process
Example: Web-Based Status Tracking

Structured Routine Process
Example: Weekly Timesheet

Automation
Example: Workflow Based Tracking

No Tracking

High ← Compliance Risk → Low

FIGURE 7.1 Efficient Data Capture

incrementally, starting with data that are necessary for creation of the core system, and then moving beyond that as the portfolio management skill of the organization increases.

RELYING ON THE BIG BANG

Systems are not built overnight. Indeed, the bulk of the learning and success of any system comes from first piloting it with a select group of users—learning, analyzing, and then acting on the feedback received. The same pilot process can be used to build enthusiasm and demonstrate success of the initiative. Indeed, if it doesn't, then is a global rollout appropriate? Parachuting any system into any organization without first understanding the existing competencies the organization already will lead to failure, even if executive support is high. It is important that a project portfolio system builds on the competencies that the organization already has. An initial broad and overambitious deployment can not only derail a single portfolio management system but also introduce pessimism around future systems. Creating a phased and structured approach to the introduction of a system is critical to its success.

NOT TYING REPORTS TO ACTION

Any reporting process must link through to actionable decisions. Without this, reports have no meaning and discussion around them lacks focus. If a report results in the outcome that everything is on target and no action is required, that is perfectly acceptable. But if no information contained in a report could ever result in action, then the report is not worth the effort invested in generating it. Reports should be tied into a decision-making process and not divorced from them.

Of course, it is important to enable those involved in projects to wallow in the data, find their own patterns, and answer their own specific questions, but the place for that is through the business intelligence capabilities tied to the portfolio management system, not the core set of portfolio reports. Adding more exploratory reports to the core set risks diluting the focus on core set of decisions that must be acted on and reduces the efficiency of the process (see Figure 7.2).

NOT KILLING PROJECTS

It is easy for projects to persist. There are many reasons to justify continued investments, but not all of them are robust. In a dynamic business

Budgetary KPI State	Definition	Action
Green	2% over budget, or less	None
Orange	2–10% over budget	Corrective plan is created and reviewed at next monthly portfolio meeting.
Red	More than 10% over budget	Review meeting is held within five working days. Project killed if corrective steps are not approved by executive team within five days of that meeting.

FIGURE 7.2 Example of Linking Key Performance Indicators (KPIs) to Action

environment, killing projects is necessary to ensure the portfolio is optimized. It is far too easy and tempting for the optimistic portfolio manager to allow underperforming projects to persist and thereby deprive other projects of funding, which would raise the performance of the overall portfolio. It is stopping and killing the weakest projects that often provides the simplest and easiest jump in portfolio performance, but inertia can prevent this. It also requires a frank and open culture within the organization to acknowledge failure and kill projects.

In addition to not killing projects, the second risk is not killing projects fast enough. Projects go off target one day at the time. Assuming that a quarterly monitoring process will spot this soon enough may be too optimistic; a project might be three months late before corrective action is taken, consuming resources that another project could have used for all of that time. Ensure that monitoring processes are as real time as you need your decisions to be. Technology makes this result easier to achieve, and the return on investment of speeding up the decision process is often a high-return investment for most organizations. In some cases, high-level monitoring may be sufficient, as there is sufficient slack that slippage can be tolerated or effectively dealt with. However, in other cases, even if review meetings are quarterly, you should ensure that you have exception-based real-time data to capture and alert you to any major changes in the interim. Exception-based reporting is critical here. Although you don't need to see every metric every day, technology can provide alerts to surface as soon as a project goes off target.

FAILING TO CALIBRATE ESTIMATES

Estimation is hard. Without a process to check the accuracy of estimates, estimates will not become any better over time. Worse, without any check on the process, estimation could become simply the political means of getting the project you want funded because there will be no repercussions for unreliable estimates. The problem, then, is worse than just poor estimation. Estimation becomes intentionally misleading. In fact, the projects with honest estimates would be less likely to get funding because their counterparts with dishonest estimates would show higher, but less reliable, return on investment. It is clear, then, that any portfolio management process requires not just a robust estimation process but, ideally, a process that tends toward self-correction and greater accuracy over time.

A range of estimation techniques can be used to improve performance. Analysis of historical data is common. No two projects or tasks are completely identical, but looking at historical data is valuable. Three-point estimation can also be used, comparing the high-, low-, and mid-point values to arrive at an estimate.

However, the key to effective estimation is not any particular technique but the introduction of a feedback loop. It is important to test estimates against outcomes and thereby refine whatever process is used over time. Postmortems can be an effective means of checking estimation and can bring a number of other process improvement benefits as well. However, the key is that a calibration process is in place. For longer projects, a postmortem at project closing might not provide the feedback quickly enough and postmortems *within* the project should be used. Estimations are such a critical and challenging part of the process that a feedback loop is essential in creating a robust portfolio management system.

MISSING SCOPE CHANGES

It is ultimately obvious if a project runs over budget. Equally, it is clear if a project is behind schedule. What can be less apparent is whether a project is truly meeting scope requirements. For example, problems with overall quality may not be apparent until long after the project is finished, or minor cuts in the amount of work done may be important but hard to detect. It is this chipping away at meeting the full scope of the project that is keeping the project on target. These scope changes can be decisive in determining project success or failure. Therefore, scope should be monitored just as carefully as budget and duration, even though it is the often the hardest thing to put into one clear single metric. Often, using more subjective metrics to capture scope can be valuable where there is not a single metric to define scope or quality. It can also help to structure projects into milestones that require customer or end-user acceptance to occur before the milestone is complete, as a built-in check to the process.

By using this milestone structure, the approval of particular milestones acts as an implicit check on the quality of the work being produced.

COMPARTMENTALIZING INFORMATION

Information increases in value as more people across your organization can see it. Locking down information or making it hard to access prevents the organization from acting as a single entity. This happens when connections across divisions and teams will not occur and duplication of work is likely to result. The worst form of compartmentalizing is having data in a filing cabinet where it can only be accessed by someone physically accessing the files—a slow and time-consuming process. E-mail is somewhat better, but it is not designed as a long-term data repository and the data can be hard to structure and access, especially for those who join the portfolio process at a later date. Creating a Web-based strategy for sharing project and portfolio documents is key and ensures that the system is open and easy to use for as much information as possible. This is helpful in enabling a truly productive organization. Sharing data in this way reduces the need for senior management to police the organization, ensuring that one group is talking to another where their agendas overlap. Providing this information in a transparent manner enables these serendipitous conversations to occur with limited managerial effort once the right process and technology are in place.

PROVIDING INADEQUATE RESOURCES

Projects don't reach completion because they have approval. Simply approving a project is necessary but not sufficient for its success. Effective completion occurs because projects get the resources they need to do the work. Lack of approval causes a desirable end to a project. Lack of resources leads to slower failure and underperformance, as well as a failure to achieve the desired outcome. Ensure that all approved work has a sufficient resource plan in place and that those resources can be met.

An alternative is to not have a resource estimate, but to commit to giving the project the resources it requires. However, this approach is risky.

Without an ability to effectively outsource and the deep financial resources, it may not even be possible, particularly where there is a bottleneck for key internal resources, and outsourcing is not an option for key strategic tasks. A simple commitment to finding the resources is unlikely to succeed. Even if only two projects within the portfolio take this blank-check approach to resource management, what if they both need the same resource at the same time? In practice, building out resource plans for all projects within the portfolio is critical to ensuring that they are successful.

The other aspect to sufficient resourcing is in terms of the tools necessary for project and portfolio management to be conducted effectively. Projects need the raw materials to be successful, but the right infrastructure is necessary for those projects to succeed. Ensuring that the organization has the right communication tools to reach other employees effectively is critical, as is ensuring that an intuitive and rich collaboration platform is available to communicate around project documents. Business intelligence tools are also critical to empower users to perform meaningful analytics on their projects.

PLANNING INSUFFICIENTLY

Planning is the key to success. It is often said that failure to plan is planning to fail. It ensures that the goals for the project are desirable and attainable. It ensures that interdependencies are identified, that estimates are reliable, and that work is correctly scoped. Ironically, a rapid and rushed start to project work is also likely to accelerate the project's failure. Investments in planning are resources well spent, given that project failure is so common. Focusing on planning might seem pedestrian in the context of portfolio management, but it is key to enabling projects to be truly productive. Effective planning can be supported by appropriate governance at the portfolio level, ensuring that the required plans are in place before project initiation.

Advance planning also enables the team size to remain relatively constant for most projects. This is desirable because rapid increases and decreases in team size over the life of project can make the project team less effective due to the disruption it causes. Predictability in team size is one of the main benefits of effective planning, but all estimates will improve, as will the scope and sequencing of the work undertaken. Planning also provides time to work with and define appropriate stakeholders, so that as a project develops and modifications are needed, the right people can be consulted and informed.

KEY QUESTIONS

- Are you rushing the process of portfolio implementation?
- Are you killing projects to free up room for new opportunities or to react to business changed?
- How are you ensuring sufficient time is spent on planning?
- How are you managing the trade-off between delivering on scope and delivering on time?

8

Communications

THE IMPORTANCE OF EFFICIENT COMMUNICATION

Communication is vital to portfolio management success. Technology is revolutionizing the way people communicate. Since so much of portfolio management is communication, the value of technological innovation here is obvious. Communication is also an area where much technology innovation is centered. The value of communication is in reducing the friction and confusion that can cause project failure. Communication is the grease that eliminates potentially damaging frictions from the project portfolio management process. Effective communication enhances the ability for coordination across the project team to quickly identify and solve problems before they have a negative impact on project performance. There are a number of ways in which project communication is improved by using technology. Of course, the technology is not working alone but is enabling your people to magnify their impact in managing projects and portfolio successfully. It is not so much changing the way they work as speeding up and creating efficiency and impact across many activities that are already occurring.

PRESENCE: REACHING PEOPLE FASTER

Presence in tools such as instant messaging enables users to instantly view whether their colleagues, suppliers, or customers are available to be contacted based on reliable data about their availability, interpreted automatically by using inputs from the user's calendar, computer, telephone, and other devices, or manually set by the user. Presence provides a single point of access to all points of communication for an individual—such as e-mail, instant messaging, personal Web sites, and phone numbers.

This makes it much easier to collect and communicate project status as well as manage project issues, because the time taken to effectively reach people is dramatically reduced. This is because all the channels for reaching a colleague are consolidated, so that if a phone call doesn't get a response, an e-mail can be written without having to look up the e-mail address—the notion of presence gives a visual indication of whether people are free or busy automatically. Therefore, you don't waste your time calling a colleague when you know she is in a meeting, and you know not to stop by someone's office when you see from his presence indicator that he is out of office that day. It also avoids the tedious business of looking up phone numbers or e-mail addresses. All contact details can automatically be kept up to date, and the risk of incorrectly typing an address or dialing the wrong number is eliminated. If someone is phoned to get status, but cannot take a phone call, she can immediately move the discussion to an instant message.

With this information, project and portfolio managers can reach people with a much higher success rate. This is particularly important in the field of project and portfolio management when frequent but short conversations are needed, and the simple act of locating people, and then getting in contact with them, takes up a high proportion of time for what are typically fairly brief but important discussions on the latest status update or issue resolution. Using different modalities also increases the response rate dramatically. If the person you are trying to contact is in a meeting, then he might not be answering his phone so e-mail can be used. If the person is not checking e-mail, then instant messaging provides another contact point.

STORING INFORMATION

Collaboration portals make it easy to store information, such as documents, online and give the right people access to them. In addition to documents, live project dashboards and project plans can be stored and viewed online. This avoids the time lost in searching for the latest project information and creates a single source of truth for the project in question. A single source of truth is critical, as often project information is inaccurate hours after it is produced, making printouts unhelpful and possibly misleading, except for the times they are purposefully created for such standing events as the weekly meeting. Outside of those times, the real-time nature of a project dashboard is extremely helpful in disseminating up-to-the-minute information. The information is stored along with automatic metadata, making it easy to see who produced the information and how recently it was produced. This makes assessing whether the content being viewed is stale much easier and avoids the need to wade through multiple versions of the same file to work out the right one to use.

Improvements in searching and indexing information also mean that information stored online can be found rapidly without having to track down the information by e-mail or search through a physical archive. These methods of information retrieval are time consuming, for both yourself and others, and if you're away from the office, then searching through a physical archive is impossible.

COLLABORATING BEYOND DOCUMENTS

The advantage of collaboration goes beyond document storage. Work is inherently collaborative, whereas documents themselves are not. Collaborative sites are versatile and can provide the tools needed to support a well-functioning collaborative team. Up-to-date lists, calendars, databases, and images can also be shared online. This gets key data out of flat documents and into a form where the team can collaborate on it. The real benefit comes into combining all of these parts into a customized intranet site related to a particular project, and these sites are sufficiently easy to build so that customization does not require IT involvement, which can slow things down or block progress for smaller teams who may not have the IT resources. The documents need not be just confined to the project plan; the recent deliverables or work in progress can be stored.

Adding images and video, based on progress in digital asset management, makes it easy to capture progress that wouldn't easily fit into a document, such as a video of the construction site making it clear how work is progressing. Or a list of the key decisions pending on the product could be posted electronically so that it is visible to everyone and can be updated as decisions are made or new questions arise. Alerts make it easy for those who care about the content on the site to be automatically notified by e-mail, or even on their phone, when content they are interested in changes.

CREATING INSTITUTIONAL MEMORY

One additional benefit of using these sorts of portals is to create an instant institutional memory for the project team. Previously, when a new member joined the team, the project manager might have to go through the archives or their e-mail inbox to find the right materials to get the new participant up to speed. Even then, with the most diligent project manager, the materials found are likely to be out of date and incomplete. Worse, other data might be scattered across different Post-it notes or stored in people's heads. Having a working online portal means that the up-to-date materials are instantly available and presented in a clear, visual format. These documents can then be easily found by those looking for the most accurate information, and they know that they can trust it. This is also beneficial when a team member misses a meeting or comes back from vacation. Having an automatic project hub makes it easier for team members to stay current. There is also benefit for executives. Team portal information is unlikely to be something that an executive monitors frequently, given the level of detail and the number of projects in the portfolio, but when questions arise, or a project slips behind schedule, an executive can use the portal to get an instant visual overview of the work occurring, without having to spend time chasing up those involved. Having this detailed catalog of information makes drill-down investigation a quicker and easier process.

This portal approach helps not just for information but also for project and portfolio risks and issues. Clear tracking of risks and issues is essential for project and portfolio success. Keeping them on paper is not reliable or transparent, and it works poorly when different people need to collaborate on solving the various areas. E-mail is a more collaborative solution, but it can rapidly lead to information overload or confuse people as to whether they are working with the latest version. With e-mail, ensuring that the right people are on the distribution is important too, and that can be a challenge as the risks and issues evolve over time. Creating a repository of risks and issues makes it possible to have the latest information in one place with full context and to grant the right people access.

CUSTOMIZING THE WORKSPACE

Customization is crucial, so that the project workspace can suit the needs of the project team and display the required information. Team sites are also easy to customize without expertise. A project manager may use a template to set up a site and then modify it, or start from a blank site. Either way, the site can be configured to the style the project manager prefers. For consistency purposes, you may require that certain key elements such as team member contact details and high-level budget and scope details are displayed on the site, but beyond that, project managers can customize to their own style. Furthermore, different templates can support best practices within the organization, with a different template supporting a PRINCE2 or Six Sigma project depending on your organizational preferences. Also, just as the site can be accessed by drilling down from the portfolio site, so can the site contain summary information with drill-down information behind it.

USING SOCIAL NETWORKING

Social networking started as a consumer technology, with tools such as My Space, LinkedIn, Windows Live, and Facebook being examples popular in North America and Europe, with the addition of Friendster and Orkut in Asia. Similar concepts are being used by firms within the workplace to provide informal means of information through one-line status updates, sometimes called microblogs. Microblogging provides an easy way for individuals to stay up to date on topics. These tools provide greater context on an individual's role and function within the organization. The value of this technology, to both the employee and the organization, is to increase the reach of what were previously informal and ad hoc *water cooler* conversations to enable colleagues who might be working on similar issues to identify overlap where there might be opportunities to collaborate or get help from a much broader section of the employee community, where previously expertise would have been much harder to identify.

This can be useful in finding quicker or better responses to existing processes and questions, but it also allows new opportunities within the organization to be identified. In this sense, social networking tools provide a much richer version of the corporate organizational chart. Now it is clear not just where individuals sit within the organizational hierarchy and what their job title is, but what they are working on currently, what they've done in the past, what their interests are, and who their key colleagues are. Previously, this valuable information could not be accessed electronically and required many informal and formal processes for the right linkages to be made.

Effective Blogging

Blogs (an abbreviation of Web-logs) can also help identify opportunities and foster enterprise-wide collaboration. Employees broadcasting what they are working on to a broad audience can help inform and disseminate information. This is a more formal version of social networking. Not everyone has a blog, since the time commitment is high and only certain individuals will have sufficient expertise. Nonetheless, subject matter experts can coordinate knowledge on a particular area or topic of interest, once again helping information flow that would have previously only come from more formal channels, if at all. Blogs can also be used to focus on particular topics within an organization—for example, more senior project managers may write biweekly blogs in order to provide a mentoring channel for their more junior colleagues, or an executive might write a blog entry to help define and reinforce the portfolio management process.

Wikis

Wikis, too, are useful in this area. They are a set of linked pages that anyone can edit, forming a radically simple database of collective knowledge. Though these tools are not created for project management, or even necessary for project management success, they are useful in a project management environment. The democratic principle wikis support in enabling anyone to edit content can be particularly useful for some areas of projects where multiple people have insight into a particular topic. Wikis involve a radical notion of trust; there is no implicit approval process and anyone with access can edit a wiki. Although this notion sounds risky, in practice wikis over time have evolved to create a powerful body of knowledge, assuming the readership of the wiki is large enough and they care enough about the topic to edit content where they see errors. Wikis can be a great tool for capturing evolving best practices, where managing the versioning or ownership of a document might prove problematic or too complex.

AUTOMATING PROCESSES

Process automation, or workflow, can speed up routine tasks. To give a basic example, time sheet data can automatically update the latest status of the project plan without the project manager having to go through the tedious process of data collection and the reentering that data into the plan. Status on tasks can also be collected via e-mail, without the project manager having to chase people down manually. All of this saves time and makes the process more robust as everything can be monitored, freeing up the project manager to focus on problems using the principle of exception-based reporting, rather than just stewarding the routine flow of data that software can automate.

Of course, complex processes involving multiple people and conditional routing and many phases can be automated, too. Examples might include implementing a stage-gate model for project approval where a project only moves through the stage-gate with the requisite documents and approvals from the right people, or an exception-based process for reviewing any project that is more than 10 percent over budget.

MOBILITY: COMMUNICATING REGARDLESS OF LOCATION

Effective executives practice *management by walking around* and spend less time sitting at their desks. Advances in mobility make it possible for the same rich experience of using a desktop PC to be available on a mobile phone, whether through an e-mail update or viewing project dashboards on a mobile browser. Technology can give project workers the opportunity to work from wherever they choose. This can increase productivity as, once again, employees can avoid the impact of waiting for the latest reporting, since the latest data can be viewed in real time—for example, by using alerts to notify executives when a key project is at risk of delay or changes in project scope occur.

Of course, mobility is not just limited to mobile phones. Laptops with seamless wireless connections are making working from anywhere a reality, and over time, changes in device formats will create hybrids on the continuum between laptops and mobile phones to create devices powerful and portable enough for almost any user. It is also important to note that the value of mobility doesn't just yield benefits in productivity, but also makes work–life balance improvements easier because people can stay in touch with work while at home and not be as wedded to the office environment, which can also lead to savings in terms of real estate cost and commuting expense.

WEB CONFERENCING: BRINGING VIRTUAL TEAMS TOGETHER INSTANTLY

It is likely that the executives supervising a portfolio will not be in the same place on the same day. Indeed, for global projects with larger teams, they may never be in the same place, but frequent and effective meetings are important for project success. Air travel is time consuming, often unhealthy for the individual, costly, and bad for the environment. Web conferencing can enable more meetings with less travel. A Web conference gives you all the tools of an in-person meeting, by using rich voice and video interfaces, and adds the ability for all to view the same document, brainstorm on a whiteboard, or use private voting to collect opinions. These tools are invaluable for distributed project teams. Web conferencing also brings new abilities to meetings, such as the ability to record the meeting for nonattendees—something that is often impractical or costly for physical meetings—and removes the need to book a meeting location. Therefore, the efficiency comes not just in greater meeting participation but lower travel costs for all involved and improved archiving of meeting content for future reference and the benefit of any nonattendees.

It is worth noting that however good the Web conferencing tool is, no software can solve the problem of different time zones for a project team with representatives in Seattle, Warsaw, and Tokyo. Widely diverse time zones make a regular meeting a virtual impossibility, and so the answer is found in multiple meetings, use of tools like persistent chat, or collaborative solutions for giving all access to the latest documents and content. The benefit of this sort of team is that progress can literally be made around the clock, if hand-offs between time zones are managed effectively. It is far from trivial to implement effectively, with cultural differences compounding time zone issues, but the truly global project team is a necessary aspect of the truly global organization.

Case Study: Communication to Build Buy-in

Stuart works out of London conducting audits for European government clients. To conduct an internal or external audit means managing hundreds of discrete projects across a broad, hierarchical team. Typically, all work is completed within a 12-month window. This process is inherently complex, especially with multiple stakeholders involved across a large government client. Effective communication of project risks and issues makes it easier for the client to act on issues faster. This is especially important because the approach to audit is risk-driven, and any issue or problem highlights a potentially significant business risk, with material consequences. The staple of audit reporting is the quarterly meeting with the finance director and the weekly meeting with the head of audit. This meeting should reach across the organization to ensure that divisional directors are aware of the issues that affect their groups, not just so that they can react to feedback and mitigate organizational risks, but also to build buy-in for the overall audit process and make it efficient and successful.

Building broad support for the audit at all levels of the organization is key to completing the work successfully. The sooner people are made aware of issues, the sooner they can react to them without waiting for notifications to come via the corporate hierarchy. Having a regular communication process that is accessible to all is important in making this work. It is important that informal channels are available to supplement the more formal reporting of results. Without effective communication, it is likely that the work would still be delivered on budget, but the use of all channels of communication provides a higher quality of service, as it becomes much easier to act on the issues raised during the process.

Communications are also critical within the project team. Using colla-borative portals to coordinate work within the team and across the organization is critical to ensuring that the organization as a whole is able to optimize performance, and so that knowledge transfer occurs as necessary.

KEY QUESTIONS

- What is your road map for implementing these communication tools within your organization?
- How will you offer training and drive excitement and usage around the tools in the context of portfolio and project management?
- Which of these tools are relatively more or less relevant to your organization?
- How are you ensuring that sufficient communication is occurring across the portfolio?

CHAPTER 9

Identifying Organizational Bottlenecks

THE PROBLEM WITH BOTTLENECKS

Every organization has bottlenecks. Bottlenecks include people who are in high demand for projects and can slow project progress because they don't have the time to complete the work required of them. Often, these bottlenecks are not identified, considering that most organizations don't complete all the projects they intend to. For example, one U.S. firm with advanced project management processes realized that the legal review was slowing its projects, even though the legal review was a fairly brief task, taking less than a day. The fact that the same handful of individuals were required to perform the same legal review on all projects, and that all projects needed a legal review, tended to slow everything down. Adding more legal staff could have cut the duration of most projects.

While the early portion of this book focused on the need to generate more ideas, it is also important to consider the bottlenecks those ideas face. If you create 10,000 ideas, do you know what stages they go through today, either formally or informally, and where most ideas are blocked within your organization? Putting more ideas through the process will proportionately increase the output, but understanding and then eliminating the problems where ideas are blocked will also help increase the innovation rate within your organization. Putting in place a clear, simple, and transparent process will help idea generation, but understanding how your innovation process actually functions today will help you move the organization to a higher level of innovation.

There are a number of ways to identify organizational bottlenecks. Identifying these bottlenecks can dramatically improve portfolio performance.

Case Study: Tracking Bottlenecks in the Navy

Brian manages logistics for a nuclear submarine group within the U.S. Navy. This presents many challenges. Submarine patrols are often long, taking the submarine thousands of miles from home base. A submarine may be in an obscure and infrequently used port in a foreign country with limited on-shore resources, relative to those available at home base.

Outside of port during a mission, as Brian says, "If you're 250 feet underwater, you cannot call tech support." Ensuring that the right supplies and resources are available is critical to ensuring that equipment problems don't lead to delays, and that the costly process of expediting part replacement is avoided. In some cases, expediting involves flying people and materials out on a plane from headquarters. To this end, Brian and his team have precise data on failure rates and replacement processes for components, making it much easier to predict demand for parts even 24 months before they are needed.

With this knowledge, it becomes possible to accurately map the demand for parts and resources into the future, and compare that against gaps in inventory, to forecast gaps and identify areas of potential high demand for particular components and skills. However, the process relies primarily on historical knowledge and clearly identifiable problems. It works well for parts and components with a track record, but newer components such as flat-panel displays introduce more risk because there is a less of a track record for these components and failure rates are therefore harder to forecast. For example, in response to the increased reliance on complex IT systems within submarines, Brian has increased his level of software engineers within his support teams. Now, rather than having to expedite a fly out to fix a technical problem on a submarine, it is possible to e-mail a piece of code, or even install it remotely.

This is one example of how having an accurate forecast of resource need can avoid the costs of delay or expedited solutions to unforeseen problems. Of course, no one can predict the future with total accuracy, but across a large number of submarines, common problems become easier to forecast, leaving the need for expedited solutions only for truly unique events. The same rigor can be applied to port servicing. Brian's team uses a detailed countdown checklist to deal with routine events: 30 days before the mission, certain tasks are completed; 15 days before, a new set of tasks is identified; and so on in the final days before the mission starts. This detailed and standardized process frees up senior management to focus on the exceptional problems and ensures that the more mundane tasks are addressed in the most efficient manner.

POSTMORTEMS

The measure of success is not whether you have a tough problem to deal with, but whether it is the same problem you had last year.

John Foster Dulles

When was the last time you read an honest and insightful postmortem of a recently completed project within your organization? Some mature and project-focused organizations perform strong postmortems and benefit from them. However, in other organizations, postmortems are not written at all, and even when they are written they are not read widely enough. Other postmortems lack any real meaning, glossing over project problems to avoid any sense of failure or culpability.

However, postmortems are the central mechanism for continual improvement of project processes. Without a feedback mechanism, such as a postmortem, any process improvement is little more than informed guesswork. Postmortems are a relatively easy way, though not the only way, to uncover organizational bottlenecks. They also provide insight in a host of additional areas beyond project management itself to organizational culture, staffing needs, customer requirements, and trends in the marketplace. The reasons for lack of postmortems are similar to the reasons for lack of upfront planning. Organizations find it hard to invest time and resources into work that doesn't have an immediate benefit in terms of driving the project forward. However, as with upfront planning, effective postmortems are critical to ensuring that portfolio management process is continually improved. Postmortems enable organizational learning, which is key to organizational improvement.

Guidelines for a Strong Postmortem Process

First, postmortems should be relatively brief. Many postmortems are not completed because of the time required to write one. Reducing the time burden should help compliance with the postmortem process. It is possible to have an insightful postmortem take a page or less. Also, bear in mind that there are two sides for the postmortem processes—first, that they are written, but perhaps most important, that they are read. Brevity helps. Once the one-page format has general acceptance, lengthening may be considered. But remember the key goals are that the postmortem always happens and that it can be quickly accessed and understood by others. Another key aspect of postmortems is cultural. Ideally, the postmortem should be written by the most senior person that has a view of all areas of the project is sufficient detail. A postmortem might also be co-authored, but it is important that the postmortem is honest and objective. A distorted postmortem process can be damaging, and a balance must be struck between giving credit for addressing problems and blaming people for not avoiding those problems in the first place.

Three Key Questions

Answering these three questions well should give you a relatively comprehensive postmortem:

1. What should we keep doing?
2. What should we stop doing?
3. What should we improve?

Given the propensity to play up project successes, it is good to aim for balance between the three areas, so that for every project success there is one thing to stop and one area to improve. That way, overly optimistic postmortems can be avoided, given that the whole value of the process comes from the constructive criticism that others can learn from, thereby improving project management throughout the organization.

Technology can help this process. If you're using a workflow to underpin projects, the postmortem should be one of the final steps in that workflow. The postmortems could all be stored in a public document library to make it easy for others to find and search for relevant content across all postmortems in the document library.

Gary Klein makes an interesting argument for *premortems* in the *Harvard Business Review* (September 2007). He argues that assuming something has gone wrong, and then discussing what might have caused the problem, is effective for preemptively addressing issues in the plan. This process can effectively predict the outcomes of future events by 30 percent. The obvious difference between a premortem and a postmortem is that a premortem occurs before a project starts, assumes a bad outcome, and analyzes the causes of the outcome. Although not a widespread process, it merits consideration as a risk management tool.

WHY A LARGER TEAM MAY NOT ELIMINATE A BOTTLENECK

Another way to avoid bottlenecks can be to expand the size of the project team as bottlenecks occur. However, this is often unsuccessful. Frederick Brookes (1995) cautions against the belief that increasing the project team size, particularly for certain types of projects, will speed up the completion date or get a project that is behind schedule back on track. There are two reasons for this: the time invested in training and the expansion of the communication network.

Adding new members to a project team generally requires training to bring those new team members up to speed, both on their functional discipline and the overall landscape of the product itself. This training not only means that the new team members spend time learning and not undertaking project work, but also that other team members who would otherwise be doing productive work will be spending time training new team members. As the end of project approaches, time spent on training can be a significant portion of time remaining on the project.

Expanding the communication network is a recognition of that as a team expands, the channels of communication expand. The number of interconnections can be found by using the group interconnection formula, which is $(N \times (N-1)) \div 2$. Therefore, a team of 10 people has 45 communication channels between people. Increasing the team size 20 percent to 12 people increases the number of communications channels from 46 percent to 66 percent. Figure 9.1 graphs this relationship.

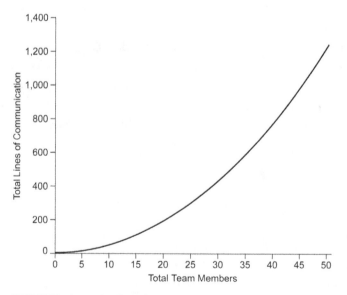

FIGURE 9.1   Increasing Team Size

Therefore, assuming instant results in productivity from increasing the project team size is too optimistic because of training needs and the resulting reduction in communication efficiency. This is important to bear in mind because team size expansion is generally considered as a last-gasp effort in the final stages of a project when deadlines are looming. The result may actually be counterproductive. Furthermore, in the final stages of a project, communication becomes even more critical. Increasing the communication network through broadening the team size puts that at risk. Hence, having a consistent team throughout the project is the ideal situation. The notion that the team can simply be expanded if the deadline is slipping in the final weeks of the project is unlikely to be a viable strategy. The expansion in communications might be mitigated somewhat if the team has multiple and efficient communication tools, but the need to supply new team members with sufficient training and context is hard to mitigate. Here, having a portal strategy to archive relevant documents online and make the past actions of the team transparent will help, but it will not solve the problem.

TRACKING BENEFITS

A related issue to postmortems is *benefits realization* or *benefits tracking*. This can be part of the postmortem process or a separate process. Were the benefits the project expected to achieve met? What were the other impacts? The exact nature of benefits tracking depends on the project in question. It may take the form of stakeholder interviews, or simply tracking financial metrics, Figure 9.2 gives a generic view of the process. Taking a long-term approach here is helpful in order to judge whether project benefits persist or are merely temporary. It is also helpful to not merely go out and assess benefits, but also to assess them against the benefits anticipated at the start of the project. This process can help improve benefits estimation, in the same iterative fashion as estimating project cost and duration. For example, benefits estimates may be too conservative in some cases, and too aggressive in others. Understanding trends and relationships here can improve all sorts of forecasting in the future, including benefits forecasting.

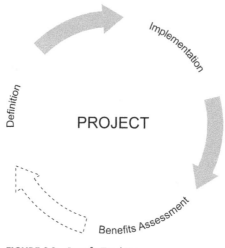

FIGURE 9.2 Benefit Tracking

Benefit management can be enhanced by workflow to make particular project outcomes more predictable and less dependent on the performance of a particular team or project manager.

Benefits of Workflow

Workflow is an important aspect of technology that can magnify the effectiveness of project management tools by including the management of processes. Rather than tracking tasks in isolation, workflow offers the opportunity to create formal systems and sequences of tasks to ensure consistent practices. This makes processes repeatable and documented. At different steps in the process specific documents can be mandated, and the approval of people or groups can be required in order for the workflow to continue. A workflow is like any other business process given its flexibility, but it gives visibility and transparency to the work taking place. Without this, it is possible to know that a project is ongoing, but it is not then possible to know what stage of the process the project is at.

Providing reporting against workflow can also provide insights into bottlenecks—for example, if proposals are getting stuck at a particular point in the proposal process. Reporting can provide this view and thereby help improve process efficiency.

Contingent Workflows

Workflows can be contingent to enable, for example, projects with different budgets to follow different approval and monitoring process. For example, projects with a very simple budget might follow a simplified workflow, whereas a larger budgetary approval requires multiple reviews. Using contingent workflows in this way enables you to reflect on how your organizational processes truly function. It avoids imposing onerous checks and balances on smaller projects, which may not be useful and can be a waste of time, and focuses more detailed steps on larger projects. Figure 9.3 gives an example of contingent workflow.

Building Organizational Processes

Workflows can also be used to keep a project on course. If a project goes overbudget, the workflow could require a review meeting and an adjusted budget to be entered into the system before future funds are

Linear Workflow

Contingent Workflow

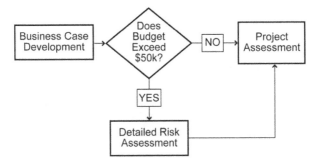

FIGURE 9.3   Contingent Workflow

unlocked. The value of using workflows in this way is that all the work can then be consistently managed to ensure that all projects go through the appropriate phases. This reinforces the ability of your organization to apply consistent project management practices and to consistently improve them.

KEY QUESTIONS

- What proportion of projects have their postmortems completed?
- What proportion of project have their postmortems read? Are you tracking benefits? Over what time period?
- Do you observe that project benefits persist, decline, or remain constant in the months and years after the project ends?
- What are you doing to capture and automate the repeated and repetitive processes within your business?

SUGGESTED READINGS

Gary Klein, "Performing a Project Premortem," *Harvard Business Review* (September 2007).

Frederick P. Brooks, *The Mythical Man-Month, Essays on Software Engineering* (Reading, MA: Addison-Wesley, 1995).

For a detailed analysis of BP's postmortem processes, termed postproject appraisals, see Frank R. Gulliver, "Post-Project Appraisals Pay," *Harvard Business Review* (March–April 1987).

For further updates on the topics discussed on this chapter, see www.strategicppm.com.

CHAPTER 10

People, the Key Element

THE NEED FOR ORGANIZATIONAL BUY-IN

Although the reasons for the failure of projects are numerous and have been discussed in prior chapters, the reasons for failure of systems and processes are generally due to lack of organizational buy-in. Lack of buy-in typically occurs when the people expected to contribute to the process don't understand its purpose, don't want to use it, or find the tool too hard to use. In an area such as portfolio management, where broad usage is necessary for success, organizational buy-in becomes all the more critical. Without broad socialization and usage across the organization, a portfolio management system will fail. Of course, focusing on the technology but not the related process and people element is likely to result in failure, and frequently does. The other factor that increases complexity is that portfolio management software and systems are relatively unique in that they require a degree of organizational change. It is sometimes assumed that a top-down executive decree is a substitute for organizational buy-in. Even in the most hierarchical organizations, this is not the case. Top-down changes are unlikely to provide a truly sustainable solution across the organization if there is not also acceptance at lower levels of the organization of those changes.

Case Study: Building Consensus for a Project Management Tool

Richard has successfully driven project and portfolio management initiatives across several multinational organizations. He successfully builds executive support while creating a network of engaged project managers. The outcome is world-class project management skills and processes across the organization. In his experience, a key aspect is to recognize and harness the multitude of project management skills the organization already has, rather than coming in with a blank-slate approach and leaning on training, or defining one singular best practice for all to adhere to. Richard emphasizes that project managers may employee a variety of different methodologies, such as Agile, PRINCE2, PMBOK, or Six Sigma, but he sees merits in all of these and encourages communication across these groups. Richard finds that this can be very effective because project managers often say, "I wish I had more contact with the PMs in group X." This inherent need for networking can create an opportunity to build a lively project management network within the firm.

Richard can build on this group of interested project managers with some light structure to foster growth and collaboration. Examples of this include the creation of a freely accessible internal project management portal with the latest academic thinking, driving mentoring for less-experienced project managers, or hosting a speaker series with leading thinkers. Bringing project managers together and exposing them to the latest research and ideas in project management can quickly spark innovation and a lead to a lot of "Wouldn't it be cool if . . . ?" conversations among project managers, especially in organizations with smart, entrepreneurial employees. From that point, it is possible to start to discuss tools and processes for realizing these ambitions.

However, Richard's processes are not solely focused on driving groundswell interest in project and portfolio management. He also provides hard facts to the senior executives within the firm who typically have a "prove it" mentality. Here, Richard launches deep, robust research projects within specific groups to define the tangible benefits of project management based on peer-reviewed academic research. This is combined with deep, survey-based analysis of particular groups, analyzing their skills in areas of project management today to the level of watertight statistical precision. This then enables Richard to have the numbers to make statements such as, "Improved collaboration on project management within this division could provide us with $20 million in incremental project delivery performance per year." That sort of rigorous analysis provides clear motivation at the executive level for enhanced project management within the organization.

Combining the executive enthusiasm with the groundswell of project manager interest gives Richard the opportunity and the means to then improve tools and processes within the organization. However, here Richard takes a flexible approach, rather than bringing in a complex system overnight. Success is once again achieved in stages, first building a central inventory of projects, with powerful, self-service, real-time reporting against it, and then thinking about the most effective portfolio prioritization process based on what the project inventory data show. He mentions that executives love the real-time data that they can easily create themselves by dragging and dropping items into a chart format or double-clicking on a particular value to learn more, rather than having to go to a business analyst with some requirements and wait days for the data to come back, as occurs with some older business intelligence tools.

Richard is also careful not to mandate too explicitly. People might come to him and say, "Give me a process," and rather than mandate a specific process, he tells them to "take the most efficient path," emphasizing the need to adapt to the situation and "expose people to different ways of thinking about projects." Richard is careful to build a process that has the core elements to support reporting across the portfolio and a consistent and readily understandable taxonomy for project information, but at the same time enables every division to customize the process to its unique business needs. Richard also looks for innovative ways for the project

(continued)

portfolio to deliver value, rather than simply improving on time, in scope, and on budget delivery. He thinks about using the portfolio data to better classify projects for tax purposes, which across a portfolio in the hundreds of millions can have a real financial impact, or the use of the organization's skilled project managers to support the company's philanthropic efforts by managing projects for nonprofits.

THINKING BEYOND THE TECHNOLOGY

Project management software is, quite appropriately, designed to improve the level of project management competence within the organization. As such, a project management implementation is not just software but part of a meaningful organizational change process and should be treated as such. Indeed, the implementation of the tool is an opportunity to create improvement across the organization. This can come through sharing best practices within the organization more broadly or from building skills that the organization currently lacks. As a result, the benefits of a project management tool implementation can be much greater than the standalone benefits of the software, and it is important to consider and plan for the opportunities the deployment presents.

ENGAGING BEYOND YOUR IT DEPARTMENT

Technology to support portfolio management is flexible. The same software can be used to support a process in many different ways—functionality that is used heavily by one organization may be used by others not at all. This is why it is critical to not just deploy the software and expect to have a portfolio solution, but also to think through the organization's goals and understand how the software can support them. This discussion is clearly a business-level discussion, and though IT must be involved, it should be working with the business stakeholders to determine the requirements for the system. Without these discussions, the risk is that the system serves the needs of IT but not other business groups and the system does not receive the recognition it needs to make it successful. In many cases, IT departments are

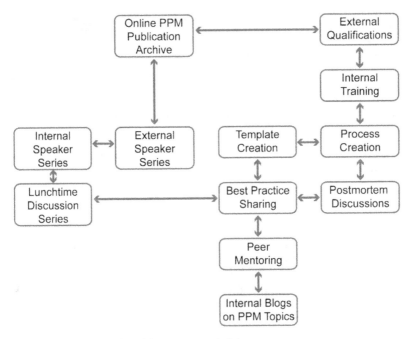

FIGURE 10.1   Project and Portfolio Management Culture

ahead of the curve with their usage of portfolio management systems, given their innate understanding of what technology can do. However, it is important that the benefits of portfolio management are communicated and used extensively beyond the IT department. Figure 10.1 identifies some opportunities for generating interest in project and portfolio management within your organization.

BUILDING YOUR OWN SUCCESS

Success of the portfolio management tool should not be left to chance. Setting up the implementation for success is critical. Repetition and early benefits will be important in driving adoption. Starting with a pilot group where benefits are likely to be realized easily will help organization adoption. This could be a group with weak performance, where there is room for improvement, or a strong group, where benefits will be smaller but the implementation will certainly go smoothly. If it is not possible to realize success with a smaller team, then success is unlikely to occur on a larger scale. The appeal of going for a group with the most opportunity might be appealing, but in the early stages, consider a group with sufficient strength that you can be assured of some early success even if the results are likely to be more moderate. Plan for these initial successes and use them to develop excitement around the system. With any change there will be skeptics, so use the initial implementation to demonstrate the value of the system. Successfully integrating the system into culture will take at least 18 months, so plan for periodic success milestones to create enthusiasm for the portfolio process.

Ideal criteria for an initial portfolio system deployment:

- The group/division stands to benefit materially and rapidly from implementing a portfolio system.
- The group/division is willing and able to provide feedback to refine the process.
- The group has systems and processes that are fairly typical of the organization as whole.
- The group is well connected with the organization, so that other teams will see the benefits of the system in action.

REPETITION, REPETITION, REPETITION

Just as demonstrating early success is a powerful incentive, so repetition aids effective adoption for tools and processes. The typical employee is exposed to about a hundred messages each day through various channels. There is no guarantee that a single message is read, let alone comprehended and acted on. There are a few ways to address this issue. The first is simply to repeat your message periodically. This is not the most elegant solution, but it can be the easiest way to achieve the desired impact. Typically, there is no shortage of initial guidance around new tools and processes, but follow-up is often limited, except on a self-service basis. Even though you may be deeply involved in the portfolio management system, for others in the organization the portfolio management system may be one of 10 other important initiatives they hear about that month, so repetition is key. Research on the psychological aspect of forming habits suggests it take about 21 days to make something habitual, if it is done daily. Less-frequent habits will take longer. Clearly, teaching people to do something once is not enough, and repeating the message in different and innovative ways over the first few months that the new process is in place will help ingrain the new concepts and ideas.

USING DIFFERENT CHANNELS FOR INFORMATION SHARING

Key to any organizational change is to teach people about the changes that are introduced. This requires more effort than is commonly assumed, and a variety of teaching methods can help success. People learn best in different ways—some prefer to read, and others to observe, learn from people they respect, ask questions, or experiment for themselves. Just providing one method of instruction will likely only appeal to a subset of your audience, and it may be a subset that is already relatively engaged and familiar with the tool. Making options available for people to learn the system in different ways is likely to improve comprehension. Provide seminars, but also provide written instruction and the opportunity to learn by trial and error. Offering various forms of training helps to improve adoption, as users can learn the system as they see fit. The usage of different channels for introducing the system also provides an opportunity for repetition, which is necessary to effectively introduce change, and it offers that repetition in a more subtle way. Using different methods of training also creates a degree of novelty, which can in itself drive interest in the changes you are proposing.

DRIVING AWARENESS UNCONVENTIONALLY

Often, some channels of communication within organizations are overused. For example, within Microsoft, e-mail is used very heavily as a communication tool. These popular channels should not be disregarded, but consider other ways of raising awareness. For example, the best awareness campaigns include advertising on tables in the cafeteria, mass voicemails from executives, posters on campus, or distributing leaflets to employees. All of these differentiate themselves from conventional communication messages and get people to actually pay attention. Using the same techniques to introduce portfolio management systems can help garner attention; the conventional means of corporate communication are likely to be less effective. The other important angle is *push versus pull*. It is tempting to want to drive awareness by bombarding employees with information, but a more savvy approach is to also demonstrate the efficacy of the system such that employees want to learn about it. If sufficient buzz and interest can be generated around the process, then it is less important to drive the message home to employees because they will seek it out for themselves.

WHAT'S IN IT FOR ME?

The most important success factor with broad adoption of any system is answering the end-users' question: What's in it for me? It is an uphill struggle if the project management tool is just perceived as additional work for the participants. There is likely to be a core group that supports any new system, but the determinant of success or failure is whether the less immediately impacted employees chose to support it. If the only aspect an employee sees of the system is filling out a time sheet once a month, it will not be surprising if compliance with the process becomes an issue, or if the less desirable outcome of forcing compliance becomes necessary. Successful implementations should demonstrate success early with a small group to encourage people to use the system, and emphasize the benefits of doing so, such as seeing the work that is going on around them, monitoring progress of all projects within the organization, and providing better understanding of how their work relates to the organization's strategic goals. Doing this will also enable pilot testing with a small group to improve the final design of the system and to ensure it is adapted to the business processes of the organization. Without showcasing benefits to end-users, adoption of the process will be much harder than it needs to be.

Area	Definition	Benefit
Capability audit	Understanding of portfolio strengths and gaps by division and group through investigation of tools and processes already in place	Understanding of the key areas for improvement and improvement within the organization, and the existing strengths to leverage
Grassroot events	Building bottom-up interest in portfolio management by encouraging collaboration and discussion between interested employees	Building consensus and enthusiasm for change at the bottom-up level, by identifying interested and motivated employees
Strategy definition	Creating the key strategic goals for the business in a concise and shareable format by executives	Sets the stage for aligning the portfolio with the strategic goals of the business. Helps to define what success means
Collaboration platform	Ensuring the organization has an appropriate set of tools for real-time document and information sharing to support portfolio management	Enables the portfolio management system to leverage collaboration tools that already exist
Communication platform	Ensuring the organization has an appropriate set of tools to support communication between employees through different modalities	Enables the portfolio management system to leverage communication tools that already exist
Tool standardization	Definition of a consistent set of tools for managing projects to make plans and deliverables consistent and readily shareable and understandable	Creates the opportunity for a consistent portfolio management platform, and limits the risk of data silos
Inventory development	Development of a single source of truth of all the projects across the organization in execution, with additional drill-down data	One place to find basic project information, and elimination of combining inconsistent or old data to obtain this view
Resource management	Consistent system for recording what individuals are currently doing and their availability to take on work in the future	Becomes possible to accurately assess individuals' ability to take on future work and automate project updates based on reports of current work
Demand management	Single source for capturing project proposals	Greater number of proposals are submitted, creating the potential to increase the overall quality of the portfolio
Portfolio prioritization	Best-in-class methodology for aligning projects with organizational strategy	Portfolio maps to strategic goals of the business

FIGURE 10.2 Example Road Map for a Phased Approach

Some examples of possible early successes to showcase the value of the system include:

- Compelling dashboards and status reports that provide an overview of project performance
- Simplification of reporting processes through usage of automatic status updates
- Improved documentation and archival systems, making project postmortems easier
- Underlying project improvements such as lower cost or faster completion
- Anything that can save time on routine tasks

THE NEED FOR A PHASED APPROACH

Phased approaches to implementation typically work best for two reasons. First, sufficient resources are available to support and train new users. When rolling out a process organization-wide, having sufficient, quality support on hand is a major challenge, and providing it may be inefficient. Second, phasing offers the opportunity to react to and learn from any feedback. The ability to react to feedback is critical and often overlooked, given the level of effort that goes into finessing the initial plan. A big-bang approach involves deploying to all users over a very short time period. This is more resource intensive, but it eliminates any problems of meshing the new and legacy processes together. Even with a big-bang approach, pilot testing with a small group before the big launch is likely, so in practice, all deployments have some aspect of phasing to them. Big-bang deployments are risky. There is no opportunity to refine or learn from the process over time, and the resources required over such a short time period are likely to be greater. Except in rare occurrences where there is the need to have everyone on the same process and the running of parallel processes during an interim period, a phased approach is recommended.

A phased approach to implementation should ensure that every phase delivers incremental value. That means that each phase should be a step toward portfolio management and have benefit in isolation and not just be overhead that will deliver value when some other aspect is implemented in the future.

KNOWING YOUR AUDIENCE

Project management tools offer different benefits for different groups within the organization. It is of little surprise that tools are best perceived and adopted by the project managers within the organization. It saves them time, elevates their status, and it is likely that they are directly involved in the process. Therefore, implementations generally work well as far as the project manager is concerned, especially where more efficient systems can drive project managers into more of project leadership role, freeing up time from routine management tasks.

For other groups, the benefits may be less obvious. What works for one group may not work for others. Importantly, just creating the reports that executives want to see will not be effective if the data are stale. Consider the team member or task owners. For them, changes could be perceived as more work, more process, or more bureaucracy. Yet this group is central to getting real data into the system. Therefore, make sure that this group is aware of the benefits in terms of collaboration that the system brings and elimination of multiple tools into one consistent process. Without getting this message right, it is unlikely that the system will succeed.

Of course, executives are key stakeholders in the process. The system should give them better access and insight into project performance within their organization, but can they access the data on their terms? Are the reports what they want to see or simply the default reports the system generates? Creating the right reports and systems to support them can dramatically improve the engagement of the executive group. There are other groups to consider, too—those who manage and assign people to projects. This might be done by management or might be a specific role. The tool should give this group an easy view to make their work quicker and easier. As Gary Cooper, an IT manager at a European utility, says:

> We are increasingly trying to benchmark projects, especially when it comes to estimating activities that are similar in size, scale, and complexity as previous projects. Executives need more information about why a new power plant build took more or less time than an identical one. Although a power plant is never identical—they're about as identical as most bridges.

LOOKING BEYOND EXECUTIVES

Portfolio management systems so often focus on executives. Of course, this would seem obvious: They make the decisions, they need the information, and, perhaps most important, they drive the funding decisions that are necessary for the system's existence. But virtually all information within the system is coming from the junior ranks of the organization, achieving the results the executives want in terms of lots of good proposals. Getting real-time project management data actually requires that the system meets the needs of just about everyone. The employees filling out their time sheets have to understand why they are doing it and see the impact; otherwise, data will come in slowly or not at all. Those submitting proposals for projects need a simple, exciting, and transparent process. It seems clear, then, that to meet the goal of giving executives what they want, a project management system must have a positive impact on everyone within the organization. Therefore, in order to truly address the needs of executives within an organization, a portfolio management system must be usable by every employee.

DRIVING MORE CUSTOMER ENGAGEMENT

Customers are often forgotten in the technicalities of portfolio management, but with better insight into project progress, that information can effectively be shared with customers. Clearly, there is a customer benefit to the extent portfolio management supports consistent and predictable delivery. In addition, greater transparency strengthens customer loyalty, ensuring that customers facing projects are truly cooperative. This is hard to achieve initially, requiring both trust and time, but the benefits of managing projects in a more collaborative way are undeniably powerful. This is particularly important for more innovative projects, where customers need to be involved to help make decisions as previously unknown constraints arise. Achieving targeted buy-in for your tool and process rather than assuming that everyone has the same needs as the project manager—or perhaps worse, that meeting the needs of the project manager is the definition of success—is setting the process up to fail. One executive I spoke with commented, "This is very important when it comes to projects that have an impact on the public or on consumer groups or NGOs. Government, partners, vendors, and suppliers are all involved, and each needs access to different levels of information."

USING TOP-DOWN VERSUS BOTTOM-UP IMPLEMENTATION

It is an oversimplification to say there are only two options to consider for a project management system—one being a bottom-up, less-structured viral adoption and the other being a top-down, centralized implementation. The approach you follow depends on your organization, and in practice, it is a continuum between top-down and bottom-up deployment processes rather than an either-or choice.

A top-down deployment prescribes metrics that must be reported and processes that must be followed. This approach creates more order and avoids confusion. It works well in hierarchical process-driven organizations. The other alternative, in contrast to a top-down deployment, is to supply the tools for viral adoption at the team level and then connect the dots to arrive at cross-division or cross organizational reporting. The approach you take will be dependent on the culture of your organization, existing portfolio management processes and tools, and the initial level of enthusiasm for the system among executive and others.

The bottom-up approach is likely to be perceived better in more autonomous organizations and relies on the benefits of the software, rather than the power of management. In many ways, this sort of viral adoption is preferable if all goes to plan, but it is potentially riskier. The weakness of this approach is in the complexity of rolling up data across different team. Although technologically feasible, creating consistent benchmarks and reporting from diverse teams for a portfolio-based analysis is harder. For any bottom-up approach, consistency between tools must be introduced early because a range of different tools can present a greater challenge in getting to a unified process than no tools at all. If using a bottom-up approach, it is useful to define some minimal aspects of a common platform or process so that the integration later in the process will be easier to attain.

KEY QUESTIONS

- Which approach is best targeted to your organization?
- What is the benefit of portfolio management for each role involved in the process?
- Which groups from outside your organization can benefit from portfolio management?
- How are you thinking about phased introduction of portfolio management tools across your organization?
- What are you doing to generate grassroots excitement around portfolio management within your organization?

SUGGESTED READINGS

For more on process value and introduction, and an insightful discussion of project management in a software context, see Scott Burken, *Making Things Happen* (Sebastopol, CA: O'Reilly Media, 2008).

For further updates on the topics discussed on this chapter, see www.strategicppm.com.

CHAPTER 11

Toward Adaptive Project Management

By Julian Tydeman

INTRODUCTION

There are multiple methods of managing projects in existence, reflecting differences in objectives, contextual settings, resource constraints, and the working styles and culture of the people involved. As befits the act of exerting control and direction, traditional approaches to project management are characterized by their clearly defined and rigid nature. The origins of these approaches are to be found in the work of men such as Frederick Winslow Taylor, who at the turn of the twentieth century brought a scientific lens to management with the goal of improving efficiency. Taking on a more thoughtful approach to management meant being more prescriptive with instructions, as Taylor described:

> The work of every workman is fully planned out by the management at least one day in advance, and each man receives in most cases complete written instructions, describing in detail the task which he is to accomplish, as well as the means to be used in doing the work. (Taylor, 1910)

141

The benefits of this more-involved method to management were evident through the productivity gains achieved. For instance, Taylor cited a study on the loading of pig iron onto rail cars, which raised an individual's output by almost 400 percent. In light of this evidence and other such work, industrial projects steadily adopted a more controlled and precise approach to management.

Since Taylor's insightful work, project management theory has evolved to incorporate a range of different dimensions, such as optimal task scheduling, stage-based completion, risk management, and standardized processes. As a whole, these developments are linked through their structured and comprehensive approach. However, in recent times an increasingly dynamic playing field has fostered the need for greater dynamism in management techniques. With many companies now compelled to be nimble in order to survive, a rigid approach to implementing strategic initiatives has become more of a hindrance than a solution. In response, more versatile forms of project management are being devised and deployed.

That said, every project management method has its benefits and place in the successful execution of enterprise initiatives. Choosing which method to use really depends on the holistic nature of the project at hand, and there is no singular best practice. Additionally, there is no need to perceive each methodology as a standalone framework, as it often makes sense to combine elements from a range of different options.

THE GANTT CHART

The Gantt chart was created in the early twentieth century by a colleague of Winslow Taylor, Henry Gantt. It is effectively a bar chart that lays out the schedule of a project. At a basic level, it shows the relationship between core activities, subactivities, and the time allocated for completing these activities.

The Gantt chart is useful in that it simply visualizes the schedule of work, allowing management and stakeholders to easily understand what tasks have been undertaken, what still needs to be done, and the time that has been allowed for each task. However, when used by itself, its capability is limited. For instance, it is difficult to incorporate an extensive list of tasks on the chart or use it to directly account for critical issues such as resource optimization and uncertainty. In light of this, the Gantt chart really is best used as a tool rather than a framework for management—although it can certainly be deployed as such in the direction of uncomplicated projects.

CRITICAL PATH METHOD

Originating in the 1950s, the critical path method aims to ensure that a project is undertaken in the shortest possible time. The method considers projects in terms of tasks, the interrelationship of these tasks, and the duration of each. With this information in hand, an entire project can be modeled in a networked sequence, probably through the use of a Gantt chart. The *critical path* is then assessed to be the series of tasks, or path, that takes the longest time to complete, thereby directly influencing whether a project meets its deadline. With this information, management is now in a position to potentially refine the sequence by arranging tasks to optimize concurrent activity and concentrate resources to reduce the time dedicated to completing the path. By applying these levers, a project can be better assured of being completed on time—or better yet, finished early.

Critical path method's strength lies in its mapping of the likely progress of a project, enabling a manager to fully grasp the scale and scope of the enterprise at hand. Although visualizing a plan can be helpful in any planning context, the critical path method is best suited for somewhat predictable projects where there is general certainty about the tasks required, their sequencing, the available resources, resource capabilities, and the time windows that will be required. Furthermore, projects that actively engage the perspective of participants in the planning process typically boost the level of certainty. A possible application for this framework could be a company that is replicating a project that has already been implemented in another team, business unit, or geographical location.

The critical path method is ill-suited for projects where there is less clarity, whether concerning objectives, required tasks, available resources, resource quality, task duration, or a combination of these. For instance, should the project objectives change in mid-flow, a manager could face the prospect of a dramatically different *critical path* and a potentially crippling handicap in the inherent sequencing of activities. Another key concern is that the method overemphasizes the tasks on the critical path that could adversely impact the conduct of noncritical path tasks. As a whole, the critical path method is not well suited as sole guidance for projects where there is a considerable amount of uncertainty, such as on initiatives new to an organization and projects with an innovative or exploratory direction.

PHASED MANAGEMENT MODELS

Phased management models are methodologies that consist of a series of distinct work stages that progress in an ordered sequence. As such, they are characterized by their logically structured and linear nature. An example of such an approach is the *waterfall model* (referring to the *flow of progress*), regarded as the classical framework for software development, which was introduced in the 1970s and comprises seven stages. In a generic sense, these stages progress in the following way:

1. Analysis and definition of the project requirements
2. Development of the plan
3. Implementation of the plan
4. Integration of all project components
5. Verification against requirements
6. Installation of the solution
7. Ongoing solution maintenance

The benefits of phased models lie in their identification of the primary processes and their clearly defined order. By allocating time to the core activities, phased models can generally assure that the critical issues in a project are addressed. For instance, the waterfall model's initial stage of analyzing and defining project requirements helps to narrow in on the customer needs to be met and the likely constraints. Additionally, by moving along a clear project road map, it is easier to build both internal and external awareness, install discipline, focus on achieving the required objective for each stage, and ensure that the baton is effectively transferred between stages.

The overarching simplicity of a phased model is particularly useful in providing cohesion and direction for large-scale projects. As a result, such models work well for bigger organizations, especially those that need to manage projects involving a wide range of functions and activities. An example might be a government organization establishing nationwide infrastructure for a new policy initiative.

The downside with phased models is that they are generally too rigid. They certainly work when all activities progress smoothly and objectives are achieved without hindrance. However, in reality, such outcomes are a rarity. More likely is that both internal and external factors will ask tough questions of and influence both the conduct and purpose of the project. In such a situation, a phased model will have difficulty in adapting to any changes in the landscape, as there are no formal processes in the model's structure to enable iteration of and deviation against the original goal. In other words, there typically is not a way to circle back and restart the process from a particular point. Additionally, the formulaic nature of a phased model encourages frontloading a project with planning activities that, from an anchoring bias perspective, further limits the ability of the project to change further along down the line. In summary, unless there is very little risk of a project being affected by macro and market developments, phased models are ill-suited for dealing with change.

EVENT CHAIN METHOD

The event chain method is an advanced derivative of the critical path method. Besides incorporating a project's implicit tasks, their interrelationship, and each task's duration, the framework seeks to account for uncertainty by enabling the modeling of task risk and the interrelationship of this risk with other risks and tasks. Individual tasks can be affected by external events, which fundamentally change the underlying state and may or may not have implications on the fulfillment of a task. When an external event does occur, it can trigger additional events both related to the underlying task and those connected to other tasks. By identifying those events or chains of events that will critically impair the progress of a project, it is possible to hedge against this risk through a restructured project plan and the deployment of contingency measures. However, identifying these critical events or event chains is a dynamic process and so requires ongoing tracking.

The advantage of the event chain method is that it helps to provide a robust project plan, enabling key decision makers to determine the relationship of risk with each project activity and thereby manage against this risk. Although calculating risk and its impact is generally perceived to be a complicated activity, the event chain method makes the analysis of uncertainty much more accessible (particularly with the use of dedicated software). Additionally, although risk quantification is ideal, the method can still work off less precise measures, such as qualitative measures. An example of where this method would be helpful is in the development of pharmaceutical products, owing to the considerable uncertainty involved in product life spans, such as with the outcome of clinical trials and regulatory approval.

Use of the event chain method is also helpful in managing expectations, both internally and externally, with regards to project outcomes. By understanding all "roads that can be taken" over the course of a project, it encourages stakeholders to acknowledge the likely or worst-case scenarios rather than just best case.

Although accounting for risk provides important detail to the conduct of a project, it also provokes a cautious mind-set, as stakeholders are likely to be unwilling to embrace those courses of action where there is a significant element of uncertainty. Furthermore, the framework entails a lot of up-front visualization work that makes it more cumbersome than helpful for projects with deliberately open outcomes or short time scales. As a result, innovative projects, with their onus on bucking trends, risk taking, and being flexible, are not a good fit for this methodology.

PRINCE2

PRINCE2 is a revised version of the PRojects IN Controlled Environments (PRINCE) project management methodology devised in 1989 by the United Kingdom's Central Computer and Telecommunications Agency. The method prescribes a holistic set of guidelines for a project's end-to-end conduct. There are eight primary processes: starting up a project, planning, initiating a project, directing a project, controlling a stage, managing project delivery, managing stage boundaries, and closing a project. Each primary process consists of the key inputs and outputs and a series of subprocesses to be undertaken (45 in total across the framework). Although originally designed for IT-themed projects, the framework is now deliberately generic enough to be used for any business function.

PRINCE2 is highly useful in providing a standardized set of best-practice procedures that can be deployed for generally any project across an organization. As such, it really is a cookie-cutter approach to project management. Consequently, no time need be wasted on establishing what processes are required, how they should be put together, and whether different teams or functions will require different approaches to achieve similar outcomes. The comprehensive structure also allows for more thorough control from a management perspective, as managers should always be aware of what activity is being undertaken and how this process is to be put together. Clearly, this latter feature has benefits from a validation and troubleshooting perspective. Additionally, as the adoption of the methodology spreads internally, organizational capabilities will benefit from the greater fluency with the language involved. In light of these points, PRINCE2 is particularly suited to large enterprises faced with the challenge of achieving consistency in the management and execution standards across their portfolio of projects.

However, the thoroughness of PRINCE2 can also be a disadvantage, as its paint-by-numbers approach can dilute the dimension of human engagement. Simply put, the directive approach of the framework can hinder the emotional attachment to a project that can develop from participants having greater freedom to contribute and act. Additionally, the methodology appears to foster an environment of micromanagement that, besides the possible adverse effect on team member engagement, can potentially stifle the quality of outcomes. Moreover, while the generic processes reflect best practices, the fact remains that cookie-cutter approaches can always be approved on in order to complement the contextual dynamics of the situation. Therefore, given the limitations of this approach, it would be unwise to heavily rely on this methodology to manage any initiatives critical to the strategic success of an organization.

PROJECT MANAGEMENT BODY OF KNOWLEDGE

The Project Management Body of Knowledge (or PMBOK) is a variation on the process-based approach of PRINCE2, albeit owned by the Project Management Institute (PMI) rather than the UK government. Like PRINCE2, it consists of a comprehensive set of generic best practices deemed essential for the end-to-end conduct of any project. However, rather than a singular framework, PMBOK offers two paths to its deployment: a core process framework (consisting of five stages: initiating, planning, executing, controlling and managing, and closing) or a core knowledge framework that focuses on particular project disciplines such as integration, scope, and risk (there are nine areas in total). These nuances apart, the benefits and limitations of applying a cookie-cutter set of processes remains.

AGILE PROJECT MANAGEMENT

Agile project management stems from a group of software development methodologies, such as scrum and extreme programming, which are typified by their highly adaptive and responsive nature. In contrast, the frameworks previously mentioned are generally characterized by their rigid and comprehensive nature that, though useful in their own way, can handicap companies with the bureaucratic and overinformed pitfalls of centralized control. In today's fast-moving business world, the ability to metaphorically turn on a dime is greatly valued, and with this in mind, some managers have begun to harness the Agilean approach for applications beyond software development.

In a Danish study based on the actual use of Agilean themes in non-software projects, the authors, Hans Mikkelsen and Jens Ove Riis, in *IPMA Project Management Practice* (2008), proposed that company agility can be achieved by applying Agilean principles on four dimensions: the creation of the project portfolio, the management of this portfolio, the management of individual projects, and the enrolment of participating resources. In the authors' minds, the portfolio of projects should center on value creation that is relevant, should be balanced in terms of risk and reward, and, as a whole, should be manageable. This portfolio, in turn, should be managed in a decisive and coherent manner (i.e., focusing on the key issues rather than getting lost in the detail). Individual projects themselves should be geared to delivering pertinent and value-creating outcomes, incorporate clear processes that engage the participants, and foster a simple and iterative workflow. Participating resources should have a broad set of skills, be capable of being switched to different tasks as they arise, and be able to translate project results into business action. As such, Mikkelsen and Riis's recommendations, and the Agilean approach as a whole, essentially prescribe the necessary effect to be achieved, leaving the means to be decided by the participants themselves.

Owing to the nebulous and somewhat revolutionary nature of the Agilean approach, its application is probably best suited to those companies with little issue in adopting innovation and change and those who have the most to gain from being nimble. Small and medium-sized enterprises heavily reliant on the use of technology in driving revenue would be a prime example.

On the flip side, it would be particularly challenging to introduce the Agilean approach to companies resistant to change, such as those with mature and established business models. A large industrial enterprise, used to deploying extensive and complex projects, would most probably prefer the comfort of a traditional directive approach rather than the more fluid and devolved nature of the Agilean method.

PROJECTS WITHOUT PLANNING—THE WIKIPEDIA APPROACH

Some projects work well without initial planning or organization. Although this is contrary to much research on why projects fail, for particular fields this ad hoc approach can be valuable. In many cases, what occurs is not the absence of planning and anarchy, but the replacement of planning by a more organic process. One example of this is Wikipedia, where there is no planning involved in specifying the articles submitted to the user-contributed online encyclopedia. There is no top-down schedule stating, for example, that an article on every type of coral will be added over the following six months. Yet articles that are submitted are then subject to an unsolicited and dynamic editing process by members of the Wikipedia community, allowing for the subject to be reviewed, built on, or even replaced by other users. In this way, regardless of the absence of a plan, the user-dependent process of review, refinement, and replacement leads iteratively to the optimal outcome over time. Really, it is this organic process that creates order in the same way that a plan would. Of course, without a plan, there is no deadline for when, for example, a certain article will be updated—or indeed that any particular article has been sufficiently reviewed for quality. Therefore, the example of Wikipedia is an interesting one: It involves trade-offs, but it makes clear that, for certain tasks, fostering ad hoc and organic activities can replace a well-specified project plan.

Of course, that is not to trivialize the Wikipedia model, as its community-generated iterative process is critical to its success. Furthermore, Wikipedia relies on technological tools such as the principle of the wiki, which is relatively new. In this case, the underlying wiki enables anyone with an Internet connection, and not necessarily a computer science degree, to edit and publish content on the site.

A CONTINUUM, RATHER THAN A CHOICE

Of course, these are not two extremes but, rather, a continuum. Any project plan that is not adapted over the life of the project rapidly becomes a work of fiction and is ignored. Also, any good estimates for an initial Gantt chart require consideration of past projects—how long they took, the sequencing of events, and so on. Also, any adaptive process cannot just begin from nowhere, but it must start with a goal and estimate of resources required and some level timeline at least for the first piece of work. Given that most organizations today leverage the Gantt-based approach more than the adaptive one, it is valuable to consider the adaptive approach and what it means for project and portfolio management. In many cases the same tools from collaboration, communication, and reporting progress are needed in both instances.

KEY QUESTIONS

* Which methods are used within your organization to manage projects?
* How do you see this evolving over time?
* How do you intend to collect the information required for portfolio management, regardless of the methodology used?

SUGGESTED READINGS

Frederick Winslow Taylor, *Principles of Scientific Management* (NuVision Publications, 1910).
Hans Mikkelsen and Jens Ove Riis, "Agilean Project Portfolio Management," *IPMA Project Management Practice*, Vol. 2 (2008).
For further updates on the topics discussed on this chapter, see www.strategicppm.com.

CHAPTER **12**

The Future of Strategic Portfolio Management

nderstanding trends in strategic portfolio management means that your process can reflect not just what is current, but also emerging trends. A system and process that can steadily improve over time and take account of new opportunities will become far stronger than today's state-of-the-art system that does not adapt. However, it is important to remember that prediction is hard—it is generally easier to predict directionally what will happen, rather than the precise timing of any development. As Napoleon said, "All plans are useless, but the act of planning is essential." Since portfolio management is a long-term process, rather than a one-off investment in technology, taking account of trends in technology is necessary so that your process can adapt to reflect them.

Although high-level, directional trends themselves can often be predicted with some accuracy, the speed or timing of those trends from early, local emergence to broader adoption is much harder to gauge.

So the way things might look in the future is possible to estimate with some level of accuracy, but how soon we might get there is much harder to finalize. Often, it is multiple trends coming together than can promote rapid change; or often innovation in one area can spill over into other unexpected areas—such as consumer trends impacting the workforce or changes in battery technology impacting portable personal computers. Therefore, the trends that follow are emerging and will continue to grow in importance, but the speed and exact nature of the changes they will create is highly uncertain.

THE CHALLENGE OF PREDICTING CHANGE—THE FAX

At the same time as looking forward, it is critical to consider how past trends and habits persist. For example, e-mail might have been predicted to replace the fax machine years ago. E-mail attachments can apparently do everything that faxing does but in a faster, more reliable way, with better archiving and the opportunity to collaborate on the documents involved. Faxing is expensive, time consuming, and with cover pages and the need to wait for a sending receipt ultimately a laborious process. But the fax remains the tool of choice for many—sometimes because of inertia, but also because e-mail has not been fully adopted as a means of exchanging legal documents, or for trading information in particular sectors of the economy where the fax thrives, and because of size constraints on multipage or graphical e-mail attachments.

There are reasons to believe that further technological advances in e-mail and other collaborative technologies will replace the fax. Information rights management will allow the sender of an e-mail to control what the recipient does with that e-mail, such as preventing edits to it. Digital signatures enable documents to be signed electronically. Bandwidth increases make it easier to send larger and larger files. In addition, every day younger digital natives, less familiar with the fax and who have grown up with e-mail, enter the workforce. The fax machine will likely become obsolete, but the fax is a good reminder that the timing of change is notoriously hard to predict.

PREDICTED CHANGES TO STRATEGIC PORTFOLIO MANAGEMENT

Several changes are likely to impact strategic portfolio management in the future. Of course, this is not an exhaustive list, and other less predictable trends will emerge:

- More fluid organizations
- Richer data
- More outsourcing
- Deeper, more extensive integration between systems
- Work management
- Seamless data capture
- Anywhere access
- Resource management
- Integration with personal task management

More Fluid Organizations

This is an important and necessary change for project management systems. Projects, almost by definition, cross organizational boundaries, whether it is collaboration between marketing, sales, and engineering on a new product launch or between a third-party consulting firm and a client on a strategic project. Projects commonly span organizational boundaries—in fact, they must in order to be successful—yet project management systems do not always reflect this. Project management systems themselves may magnify this trend. As organizations become better at identifying areas of expertise and common interests, so projects will increasingly span different groups and even companies. Search, social networking, and other tools will increase the span of information to enable people to collaborate effectively, whereas previously they would not have known of each other's existence.

Today, most projects are cross-division and many go beyond a single organization to encompass an entire supply chain or many vendors with unique skills to bring a particular product to market. However, security concerns or administrative complexity often prevent the project system from spanning the entire process. Usage of consistent systems will enable organizations to move beyond ad hoc sharing of project information using e-mail to more fluid communication based on shared access to a common system, with role-based administration used to maintain confidentiality of particular projects or sensitive financial or personnel data.

The main trend here is for project management systems and collaborative tools that underpin them to catch up with the way people work. The technology is there today, but organization's security and administrative processes will be slower in adapting to these changes. This is often for good reason, since effective security is a cornerstone of the system, but this should not compromise the right people sharing the data they need to get things done on either the project or portfolio level. The usage of project management tools spanning the supply chain is common in the automotive sector, as is collaboration between different firms of subcontractors on construction projects, where tens of different firms are involved. It is likely that this collaborative approach to projects and portfolios will spread beyond just this industry.

Hosted versions of software applications may accelerate this trend. A challenge with sharing access is that if the portfolio management system exists behind one organization's firewall, then granting access to others is complex. If the portfolio management system is hosted over the Web, often referred to as being in the cloud, then access is more democratic. All organizations can access the system on an equal footing without it being behind one organization's firewall.

Another angle to the fluid organization is greater versatility within and across its own divisions. Today, the process of matching people to projects is quite narrow within many organizations. Sometimes, word of mouth is used to find the right people. Occasionally, a search might span a particular team or even a division. However, creating a transparent project staffing model can help broaden employee's opportunities and match the right people to the right project role with greater success. Today, most organizations succeed at transferring people to different jobs within the organization to broaden their exposure. Indeed, Japanese firms are experts at this process of developing the skills of their employees through rotating them through different positions. However, this model often applies to a discrete job and not to particular projects or assignments. Just as organizations blur the boundaries that projects are managed across, so employees will enjoy more free agency within the organization and be able to create their own job description based on set of projects they are suitable for rather than predefined and static job title.

Richer Data

Data on project performance need not be confined to formal metrics, such as a status indicator set periodically by the project lead, but, rather, can be pulled from disparate sources across the organization to identify trends and patterns where previously the data just were not available. There was not the means to capture data, as the process of doing so would have been labor intensive, or storage constraints made the archiving of large sets of data without a compelling and immediate business benefit hard to justify. This abundance of data means more insight but also more false signals. In addition to capturing data, setting appropriate thresholds for reaction and structures for analysis will be key.

One example of this is capturing historical data from the system to enable a database for project postmortems. Rather than relying on subjective data for assessment of project performance, projects can be compared to past projects with similar characteristics. This richer dataset can then inform a superior estimation going forward, with historical data acting as a cross-check on individual's estimates; as the repository of completed projects grows, so the project repository becomes more informative. Organizational learning can be enhanced, as what works at the portfolio level can be tested, proven, and repeated, while superfluous processes can be modified or killed. The analysis of meaningful data can lead to further improvements over time and continual improvement at the portfolio level.

SIGNAL TO NOISE RATIO

It helps to think of data in terms of the signal to noise ratio, where a *signal* is useful information, such as a correlation between sales and the weather or knowledge that high-value customers spend $70 more per month than low-value customers. *Noise* is just mounds of data that take time to look over but don't yield any conclusions, actions, or insights. Managing the signal to noise ratio is key, and as the volume of data increases, having clear patterns and metrics for analysis will be all the more important.

More Outsourcing

Outsourcing is happening today as the frictions in contacts between organizations decline, global communications become more seamless, and specialization of a particular organization on a specific task increases. Most projects contain team members external to the firm. This happens when team members are suppliers, vendors, or consultants. Of course, every piece of outsourcing is itself a project at least containing a request for proposal (RFP) and probably much more. Therefore, as with anything else, capturing all of this work within the portfolio will be key. Outsourcing also increases the need for virtual teams and collaboration beyond the boundaries of the firm. Efficient monitoring of key performance indicators (KPIs) will be increasingly important as a contractual way to measure the effectiveness of outsourced projects and provide a common and agreed to framework for measuring success. As more outsourcing occurs, it is likely that the different participants on a project will be in different organizations rather than different divisions of the same organization, so cross-organization collaboration becomes all the more important, whether it is across time zones, cultural boundaries, or organizational hierarchies.

Deeper, More Extensive Integration between Systems

Project management involves many different tools to be effective. For example, many projects start because of a sale, or even during the RFP process, so integration with your customer relationship management (CRM) system is important for many organizations. Links to the enterprise resource planning (ERP) system are also critical for capturing the latest budget data, and that process will become more automated and seamless with the addition of master data management strategies for ensuring that the codes and taxonomies applied to projects and project data are consistent across the organization. Other project needs may arise from dashboarding tools. If a process becomes too slow or inefficient, a project is needed to fix it and the dashboard review process can trigger that project request—first as a smaller, investigative project, and then as a more formal process.

From a user perspective, it is important that the collaboration tools for project management are consistent with the other tools being used across the organization. This is increasingly important for collaboration tools such as e-mail, instant messaging, voice calling, or persistent chat. This functionality will increasingly be integrated with the project management tools so that there is no need to leave the project status plan to phone the project manager—a simple click on the individual's name launches a choice of ways to connect. Indeed, this is increasingly possible even today.

Ultimately, we must achieve a situation where the whole notion of integrating systems is not even something the end-user notices. The transition from one system to another feels completely seamless to the end-user, and the need to complete one task in one application and a second task in another is no longer even an issue. This will reduce training costs across the organization, as the need to learn multiple tools declines and features and functions become naturally discoverable from within the application, rather than from an instruction document or a training seminar.

Work Management

All projects are work, but not all work is a project. This means that portfolio management systems are hampered because they cannot see all work within the organization. Applying some of the discipline of project management to ad hoc work within the organization can offer the benefits of project management to all employees within an organization.

For example, avoiding duplication of effort can be extremely valuable for small projects as the chance of two separate work streams working toward the small goal is high. This is particularly true in the early stages of new ideas, when the topics being worked on may not have been shared broadly within the team or group. Small projects often lack visibility and transparency, which means that they are not as discoverable. This can be a problem for those in the organization who are interested in the work being done, or could offer solutions to problems. The prevalence of small projects also means that resource management is less effective. An employee who works on a major project has that portion of time captured in full, but the 20 percent of his time spent on a smaller project does not appear in the system or the reports it generates, creating the illusion of spare capacity. This is an illusion because, in reality, the employee is at full capacity—it is just that the 20 percent of time spent on a smaller project is not captured.

As Figure 12.1 shows, holistic vision of work management can offer these benefits. The challenge is capturing the work done on these smaller projects in a simple enough way that it can easily be rolled up for reporting purposes and the burden on the project team to report is not too onerous. Capturing all work also leads to a superior strategic alignment process. Of course, the largest projects are likely to have the greatest strategic impact, but the mass of smaller projects, if captured and analyzed, can help complete the picture and ensure that all projects are contributing to the organization's strategic goals. For example, if a strategic goal of the organization is to build deeper customer connections, it might be that no single project can do this, but that hundreds of small projects all focused on a particular customer with a handful of employees can. Capturing these projects may be seen as too much overhead, but if the process is sufficiently lightweight and easy, then rolling these projects up will provide a comprehensive view of the work that is being done.

Seamless Data Capture

Project systems most commonly fail due to out-of-date or stale information. Stale information can be more dangerous than no data at all.

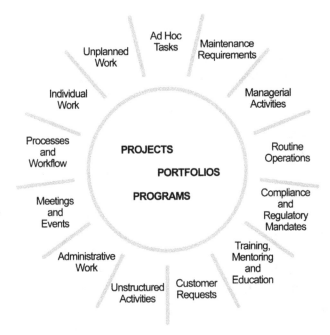

FIGURE 12.1 Work Management

This can occur when pain of collecting the information is greater than the incremental value the information provides, and the need to collect project data on a routine, weekly basis gets sidetracked by the time pressure of urgent, "real" project work. In some sense, this view misses the forest for the trees—a project that loses its high-level performance tracking and executive visibility is at greater threat of failure than any single project issue might present, but it is the day-to-day issues that are more pressing and apparent.

This is true in any field, but the problem is felt particularly keenly in project management. The average project is months in duration, and data that are even a week old can mean the difference in being on track or behind schedule and thus can delay corrective action. The key to project management is forecasting the future in an unbiased and consistent way. This is challenging even with the latest data, but without the data, the project itself is in jeopardy. Of course, all data systems work better with real-time information, but for projects the benefit of being current can have a much greater impact on performance.

This eternal challenge of gathering accurate project management data creates many opportunities for technology. In the same manner that communications tools now capture *presence* of the information worker without them having to take any action (e.g., by inferring data from the individual's calendar), so project management tools could automatically update status plans based on rules-based engines applied to meetings held, documents submitted, or e-mails exchanged. Once refined, these tools provide the opportunity to both free project team members from the burden of status reporting, but also perhaps provide greater insight than individuals themselves would be able to report. For example, someone's estimate of how long a particular work item took might be less reliable than an estimate based on a machine-based measure of the time the user was actually writing the document on her computer. Privacy concerns will rightly limit data that can be collected and the process will be opt-in, but employees might like the freedom from having to report their time if the system automatically collects it for them. The goal would be to save individuals time on laborious overhead processes, such as completing a time sheet or reporting status on their tasks each week. The resulting data may also help individual efficiency if they can see how effectively or ineffectively their time is spent.

Workflow provides a window into how this scenario might evolve. Today, rules can be generated when documents are posted or approvals happen. It still requires some level of user intervention to start the process, but the work is minimal and the updates are seamless. By using workflow and simplifying processes, the likelihood of capturing more and more accurate project data is enhanced and time is saved on the repetitive process of pushing data around, which can now be freed up for more productive activities.

Anywhere Access

Project data will increasingly be accessible remotely, through multiple devices from any location. For example, the executive can view the latest project dashboard on his mobile phone and then drill down on a project with budgetary issues to contact the project manager concerned. The project team member can fill out his time sheet from any device with an Internet browser. The customer of the project can get real-time updates on any scope changes.

Advances in security will further bolster the ability for those with the rights to access data to view it from wherever they are using any device, and to make the experience across those devices seamless. It will not matter if you last edited your project plan on your laptop; when you next pull up the details of the project dashboard on your cell phone, the data will be synchronized to it. It is interesting that the prophesized device convergence has not happened yet. The number of devices people use is proliferating both in the workplace and in the home, with many people owning multiple laptops and desktops, and some people even owning two cell phones to keep their work and personal life separate. However, the opportunity to synchronize all types of data and content across those devices in real time is becoming a reality, and the benefits to portfolio management systems where real-time data become the lifeblood flowing through the system is clear.

Anywhere access and synchronization across devices is sometimes viewed as a threat to people's time when they are not at work, forcing them to be responsive to requests and challenging the balance between work and personal life. However, more optimistically, anywhere access to project information creates the freedom to avoid unnecessary commutes and travel to meetings, while still remaining productive outside of the office environment. This creates the opportunity to spend more time on key objectives, such as meeting with customers without being disconnected from core business issues, or simply to waste less time and resources commuting and eliminating the need to take physical documents with you when you're out of the office or worrying about whether they are up to date when you do leave the office unexpectedly.

Resource Management

Project staffing often contributes to many portfolio management problems. Project may get delayed as a resource is in demand for other projects and is not available to complete a task on the required date, hence slowing the project. In addition, many projects that are approved are not done because the resources are not available. Sometimes a resource that appears very suitable for a project turns out not to be suitable and the project is delayed while a substitute resource is found, and often some rework is required.

Project management systems, in conjunction with social networking–style tools within the enterprise and improvements in search, will enable identification of people suitable for a particular project role. This enables a richer form of people search than using existing job descriptions and formal corporate hierarchy to find the right people for projects. For example, two software developers may have the same role and tenure, but one is very familiar with a particular software programming language whereas the other is not. Knowing the requirements of the project, and then having a richer way of capturing expertise, will enable more efficient matching of resources to projects. A richer method of capturing expertise, based on pulling data from people's actions and history, with their approval, will enable creation of a much more informative definition of workers' skills, which will be invaluable to larger organizations as they look to staff projects efficiently and leverage the skills of all their people to get more done with fewer people and re-sources. Today, this information exists in people's heads and is invaluable but documenting it will make the process quicker and more robust.

Integration with Personal Task Management

Today, personal task management systems are seldom used, and they are rarely integrated with project management systems. There is a need to bridge this gap, which will help both the individual and the team work more effectively. Ultimately, any work items require the individual to take action.

Personal task management tools, which may be integrated into e-mail, help individuals manage and prioritize all of their work, even where it is not part of a larger project. In addition, systems such as David Allen's Getting Things Done (GTD), which is a theory of managing an individual's tasks, rather than a software product, provide a richer system for management of an individual's work (Allen, 2002). The focus of these tools is on the individual and helping them manage their diary, tasks, and appointments. This individual focus means that these tools do not focus on holistic team management. However, they help an individual capture and log her own tasks in a complete and comprehensive fashion.

In the future, it is likely that these tools will become more integrated with project management systems. Today, information can be pushed down from project management systems into these tools and real-time updates can be applied to the project plan automatically based on how work is progressing, but little information is rolled up to surface individual work at the team level and to eliminate duplication of effort and facilitate conversations between individuals, who may be working on similar topics but are not aware of it. This is particularly acute for small tasks, which may not be part of a broader project plan. If these smaller tasks are not tracked, individuals will have trouble managing their work and resource management becomes challenging because availability is less meaningful if someone appears free but is spending time on work that is not captured in the portfolio system.

KEY QUESTIONS

- How will you take advantage of advances in portfolio management as they arise?
- Which changes are most relevant to your organization?
- Where are the opportunities to integrate with advances in other areas of your organization?

SUGGESTED READING

For a description of the Getting Things Done method, see David Allen, *Getting Things Done* (Penguin, 2002).

Conclusion

Portfolio management requires a combination of the right processes and the right technology to support it. Portfolio management is a process. This process must improve over time. Without improvement, any process, even if state of the art at the time it is introduced, will eventually become overly bureaucratic or outdated. For this improvement to occur, building feedback into every stage of the process is critical. There are several key initiatives that will dramatically improve your ability to execute effectively on a strategic portfolio and continually improve on that execution over time.

Set bold goals for both the business, and therefore the portfolio, and share these goals repeatedly and broadly.

Just setting aggressive goals can help performance, but combining it with a portfolio approach magnifies the power, as there is a visible and robust link through to execution. Without this linkage, the value of strategic planning can be wasted due to poor execution caused by misunderstanding at the implementation level. However, before execution can even begin, bold strategic goals must be in place.

Collect far more project ideas than you can execute on, from as broad and diverse a group as possible.

There is a lot of creativity within your organization that may not be harnessed to its full potential. The more ideas you capture, the easier it becomes to select a subset of projects that are diversified from a risk management perspective and have strong business impact, in addition to financial returns. The shorter your project list, the less likely it is that you can effectively and efficiently execute against the goals for the business. Also, understand all the stages that the proposals pass through. Lack of sufficiently creative ideas today may, in part, be due to lack of the ideas, but it could also be due to bottlenecks in the submission process that are causing good ideas to be lost. This is one example where first auditing your existing processes can help you understand how to make your idea submission process more effective.

You must manage your portfolio *as a whole* against your strategic goals for the business.

Looking at projects in isolation, or even subsets of projects on a group or divisional basis, is ineffective from a risk management perspective. It is incomplete from a resource management standpoint and may mean that only particular, specific goals are focused on, rather than a broad set with broader business impact. Portfolio management should be as comprehensive as possible to be effective.

Estimate key project parameters early and improve on those estimates over time.

Estimation is the first opportunity for the portfolio to go off course, especially because it is such a challenging phase of the process. Accurate estimation requires understanding—not just the resources required for a particular task, but also that the scope of that task is appropriate in the context of the end product for the broader project. It is also important to use range-based estimation techniques so that people don't lock in on particular numbers too early, where the psychological biases of anchoring can mean that the estimates fail to converge on their true values.

Share portfolio information broadly with as many employees as possible.

Conducting portfolio management in this way is a valuable step toward achieving a transparent organization. Truly democratic sharing of information empowers employees to make informed decisions. Without broad and transparent information dissemination, it is challenging for junior employees to make the right decisions without time-consuming and wasteful processes of working through the corporate hierarchy—arguably an inefficient use of their time, as well as the time of more senior employees, when the information could have been more broadly shared in the first place. Sharing information also creates engagement in the process, avoids duplication of effort, and promotes cooperation between teams. Cross-division opportunities are likely to be more visible when information is broadly shared. The benefits of creating a transparent organization are not just limited to portfolio management, but this is one area where the benefits are acute, and if you need to make a shift toward greater organizational transparency, portfolio management is a good place to start.

Monitor and report on the portfolio with a view to faster and more effective decision making.

The goal of reporting is solely to make decisions on the data—otherwise, it is a glorified waste of time. Projects typically go off course incrementally. Any delay to decision making often translates into a delay for the entire project. This can be enormously costly and easy to avoid. So portfolio reporting should be comprehensive, frequent, and action-oriented. Business intelligence systems should support this process, enabling data wallows and drill-downs to underlying information from more detailed reports. However, the core of portfolio reporting is frequent, automated, and actionable reports—these form the backbone of a well-scoped portfolio management process.

Track everything that is consuming resources, and go beyond formal projects to anything that is a meaningful piece of work or use of resources.

This makes prioritization efforts more robust. The more you can track, the more you can manage. Targeting your large projects is a natural first step with a portfolio management system, but ultimately widening the net to capture more work is valuable as long as the burden of information capture is manageable. Many large projects may start as small below-the-radar projects and need attention to get the right level of resourcing; other projects may have valuable links to other key efforts in the portfolio, and giving them greater prominence through a portfolio system is advantageous. The more of your organization's work you can capture, the more you can manage and optimize on a portfolio basis. Creating usable tools and systems for low-effort tracking here is important. The reason much of the data are not visible is because of the complexity of tracking tasks where no formal project manager is assigned. The more you can lower the cost and effort of tracking work, the more valuable your portfolio system becomes.

Drive communication across everyone involved in the portfolio.

Transparency is the key to this, as is having the right tools in place to support communication using different methods—from phone to e-mail to instant messaging to internal blogging by subject matter experts. Not everyone learns in the same manner, so having different channels for sharing information can help the understanding and adoption of the overall process. Reinforcement is also key to effectively introducing a process.

Support extensive planning beforehand and postmortem processes afterward.

Planning is necessary for project success. Postmortems are necessary for ongoing portfolio improvement. A postmortem process has many benefits, but keeping your estimates on target is a critical value of conducting postmortems. Without a mechanism for keeping estimates honest, it is likely that estimates will become less accurate over time, and this may undermine the portfolio management process. The key for postmortems is that they are produced consistently. Performing postmortems on only the less-successful projects is methodologically flawed. To that end, postmortems should be relatively simple processes, capturing the key elements required for project improvements with the conclusions broadly shared to promote team learning and process improvement.

Recognize the portfolio management skills that your organization already has.

Some organizations believe that they are a blank slate for portfolio management. That is often an oversimplification. Recognizing the skills your organization already possesses and leveraging them for implementation can be very useful for portfolio success. These efforts need not all be in place across the organization, but transferring existing best practices from particular groups to the broader organization can be key to reducing the complexity and learning associated with introduction of a portfolio process.

Keep everything as simple as it can be.

Examine and cut processes regularly. This is necessary to counteract process growth without you taking any action. It is often easier to add a new process than to cut an existing one, but both are necessary to keep the portfolio process in balance and to avoid bloat. Requests to add new processes will come naturally if the process is visible, people are engaged, and the postmortem function is working well. Opportunities to cut or remove portions of the process are just as important but may not emerge as frequently through the process, so make sure time is spent focusing on things to cut in addition to things to add.

Index